THE PROVIDENCE OF
GOD

THE PROVIDENCE OF GOD

Georgia Harkness

ABINGDON PRESS
NEW YORK   •   NASHVILLE

THE PROVIDENCE OF GOD

Copyright © 1960 by Abingdon Press

Library of Congress Catalog Card Number: 60-6932

Scripture quotations unless otherwise noted are from
the Revised Standard Version of the Bible and are
copyright 1946 and 1952 by the Division of Christian Education of the National Council of the
Churches of Christ in the U.S.A.

SET UP, PRINTED, AND BOUND BY THE
PARTHENON PRESS, AT NASHVILLE,
TENNESSEE, UNITED STATES OF AMERICA

CONTENTS

INTRODUCTION

MANY THOUSANDS OF BOOKS HAVE BEEN WRITTEN ABOUT GOD, AND the goodness of God has been the recurrent theme of the religious spirit through the ages. Then why another book? The answer lies in the fact that there have been few treatments of what is the "hot spot" of the issue for the modern mind—the relation of divine providence to human acts and choices and to the world of natural law and orderly uniformity within which our lives are set.

There is no dearth of books on the general theme of the relations between science and religion. Since the appearance two generations ago of Andrew D. White's monumental two-volume *History of the Warfare of Science with Theology in Christendom*[1] the warfare has abated considerably among the informed exponents of both science and theology. Few Christian leaders today contend for a six-day creation and a literal reading of the first chapters of Genesis, and evolution has been generally accepted as the process by which the eternal God over many millions of years has been fashioning His world. But this does not settle all the issues.

The points at which there is still great uneasiness among many Christians center about the efficacy of prayer, particularly petitionary and intercessory prayer, the possibility of miracle, and the reality of God's providential guidance and care in events that seem enmeshed in a network of causal relations. To these may be

[1] New York: D. Appleton Co., 1898.

9

added another in a related but somewhat different dimension—personal existence beyond bodily death. On the one hand there is the indisputable biblical testimony, reinforced by centuries of Christian faith and witness, that God *does* answer prayer, work miracles, shape events according to His loving purpose, impart eternal life. On the other there is the scientific modern temper permeating the whole of life and telling Christians, as well as others, that every event must have a cause within the natural order and that there is dependable knowledge only of that for which there is empirical evidence. The result is the complete rejection of belief in providence by some, while others cling, often too naïvely, to a type of faith in providence that to the sophisticated looks like sheer credulity and wishful thinking.

These matters constitute far more than an academic question. I have dealt with students for many years and do not feel discouraged about them. Many are concerned with the claims of their environment more than with the Christian faith and are at least outwardly indifferent to religion. Yet on almost every campus there is a devoted minority who take their religion seriously. In matters of personal religion and corporate worship, if not in social action for a "brave new world," they are on the whole more interested than were the students of their parents' generation. But the same old questions persist. God may be believed on philosophical grounds to be personal, but how can He be "personal to me"? How can the Creator of this vast universe pay any attention to each individual of the whole human race? When I pray, does this do any more than make over my own personal attitudes? If I pray for someone else, does this do anything except to increase my desire to help him? Aren't miracles simply something we don't understand but may sometime? What do you do with the miracle stories in the Bible, such as the resurrection of Jesus? How can my personality or anybody's continue after the body dies? The questions go on and on, and most of them are sincerely and honestly put.

Not infrequently one encounters the disastrous effects of an inherited faith too rigidly held. I have among my papers a letter sent to a chaplain by a young woman whose brother had been killed in the second world war. It runs thus:

Right now I just can't take sympathy or moral platitudes such as "God knows best" and that it is His will. Such is not so, and with David's death goes my entire faith in prayer. Almost every hour, certainly every day, I've prayed earnestly that God would send him back to me. He seems to have laughed in my face and belied such promises as "Ask what ye will believing" and "if ye have the faith of a grain of mustard seed." What a sucker I was to believe all that! I'm bitter and full of hatred because they murdered the one person who was dearer to me than my own life. I shall not mention it again, so let's consider it closed.

Of course, the matter was not closed! It was rankling deep within her spirit, crushing her faith and crippling her life to make a double tragedy. A truer understanding of the way in which God answers prayer and delivers us from evil might not have averted the first tragedy of young David's death, but it could have saved her from the second.

It is difficult to say to what extent the Christian hope of eternal life is still a living faith in current society. We still have for the most part funeral services in which it is affirmed. It is so much a part of the traditional patterns of thought that doubtless many accept it without any clear grounding in Christian faith. But certainly many no longer believe in the possibility of life after death, or at best wistfully hope for it when their loved ones are taken from them but with no real sense of assurance. This lack of assurance is by no means limited to the secular world and is found in the minds of many Christians. Such uncertainty has various sources, but not the least of them is the prevalence of a climate of thought which assumes that we can have positive knowledge only of that which is open to scientific verification. Under this assumption our biblical and historic faith in eternal life through the goodness and power of God stands unsupported and hence is doubted or denied.

11

Intimately connected with these problems of prayer, divine protection, and eternal life is a permanent issue of Christian faith which has been brought to fresh acuteness in our day. This is the age-old problem of evil.

In spite of the emergence of some significant modern theories we are no nearer to "solving" the problem of evil than were our fathers. Let it be said at the outset that this book will not solve it! If the reader hopes to find here a full solution, and in particular, if he expects to find an answer to the question that perennially emerges in the presence of suffering, "Why did this happen to me?" he had better lay down the book. If he persists, he will discover that the author thinks there is a better way to approach the understanding of God's providence.

Yet the problem of evil must not be evaded. Its persistence is evident not only in the ancient philosophical drama of the Book of Job but in its modern restatement by Archibald MacLeish in his poem and Pulitzer prize-winning play, *J.B.* Though I shall not attempt to enter into the controversy which has developed about this production, its author states with great vividness the problem of the relation of God's providence to the massive human suffering of our time. He writes:

No man can believe in the imitation of life in art who does not first believe in life itself, and no man can believe in life itself who does not believe that life can be justified. But how can life be justified in a time in which life brings with it such inexplicable sufferings: a time in which millions upon millions of men and women and children are destroyed and mutilated for no crime but the crime of being born in a certain century or of belonging to a certain race or of inhabiting a certain city: a time in which the most shameless and cynical tyranny flourishes, in which the ancient decencies are turned inside out to make masks for cruelty and fraud, in which even the meaning of the holiest words is perverted to deceive men and enslave them? How can we believe in our lives unless we can believe in God, and how can we believe in God unless we can believe in the justice of God, and how can we believe in the justice of God in a world in which the innocent perish in vast meaningless massacres, and brutal and dishonest men foul all the lovely things? [2]

We shall be dealing in this book not specifically with the problem of evil but with the goodness of God in its wider context. Yet let none suppose that the providence of God can be affirmed in disregard of these stern realities! These things exist, and Christian faith must reckon with them. It is hoped that some light may be thrown in the pages which follow.

It is not solely in the presence of gigantic evil that the providence of God becomes a matter of concern. No one needs to be reminded that there is a great inner uneasiness and insecurity among millions of outwardly comfortable, well-educated, and otherwise "well-fixed" individuals. The prevalence of drinking, divorce and broken homes, nervous breakdowns and other forms of mental disturbance, the vogue of books that offer cheer and self-confidence, the popularity of psychiatric treatment, and the sordidness of the stories to which any pastoral counselor must listen are ample evidence. Even the much-talked-of return to religion and increase of church attendance, though one may rejoice in it, may yet be viewed as symptomatic of a psychic uneasiness that will "try everything once."

This situation is obviously derived in part from unsettled external conditions. Years of war, with their separations and tragedies, the continuance of the cold war with the ever-looming danger of a third and all-destructive world conflict, the sharp competition, regimentation and economic pressures of modern life—all these have had their effect on the individual's inner security. Christian faith is not all that is needed to rebuild and establish it. Nevertheless, with a deep-rooted, intelligent Christian faith in divine providence these strains could be met. Without it they are not likely to be met.

Yet this is not the whole story. There is a reflex relation in which the loss of personal inner moorings is not only an effect

[2] Archibald MacLeish, "The Book of Job" in The Christian Century, April 8, 1959 (Vol. LXXVI, no. 14), pg. 419.

13

but a cause of social instability and unrest. Racial tensions break out with greatest virulence where personal emotions of fear, hate, and distilled prejudice are unchecked by a sense of divine guidance into ways of love and understanding. Wars are fought with vitriolic hatred and unbelievable atrocities are committed either where there is no sense of divine guidance and restraint or where this is perverted to a hallowing of human hatred and cruelty in the name of God. Political chicanery and the lust for power on the one hand, lethargic acquiescence in preventable evil on the other, are found where there is no strong sense of divine leading or responsibility to the Lord of history.

There is more than an accidental connection between the atheism and the tyranny of Communism, for where there is no sense of divine providence, either as *caring* or *commanding*, the State, the Party, or the dictator becomes a substitute for God. Then all the resources not only of physical but of social pressure, with its rituals and mind-molding agencies, enforce its (or his) edicts. This is easy to see as one passes judgment on Communism from a land where Communism is unpopular; it is not always so evident that the same forces operate even in a supposedly free society when the inner attitudes that affect political action become divorced from trust in and responsiveness to God. Speaking of modern man's loss of faith in a supernatural personal God who makes unconditional demands and gives meaning to life, Herbert Farmer indicates significantly the connection between an exaggerated nationalism and monistic naturalism:

For, without the sense of being related to the supernatural personal, man sooner or later becomes conscious of being merely carried along in a flux of events, of whose ultimate outcome he can form no connection in terms of his own interests and deeds. The rise of dictatorships is related to this attitude of mind . . . the Eternal as the supernatural personal reveals itself to the heart of man through an unconditional demand, and only through his response to this unconditional demand can man be released from the process and given a truly personal life. If this is lacking, there is nothing in the end but an

14

intolerable emptiness and hunger for his heart; with the result that, seeking escape, he is ready to seize on the figure of a national leader or a political dictator and make *him* the supernatural personal, to whose demands unconditional obedience must be given, for whom, if need be, there must be readiness to die.[3]

America has not reached this stage yet, and with wise Christian leadership in political as well as religious circles it need not. Yet if there is any realism in these words, it is evident that the motto, "In God we trust," is more than conventional verbiage. As a people we *must trust* in God, which is to say we must have a living faith in divine providence both as ultimate security and unconditional demand, or we shall see both personal stability and our free social institutions jeopardized to the point of disintegration. The issue is as serious as that.

But can we put a live meaning—a meaning which has both Christian vitality and intelligent credibility—into what used to be referred to as "the mysterious dispensations of Providence"? The mystery we shall certainly not expect to remove; it is integral to the nature of the Divine Holiness to be the *mysterium tremendum et fascinans*[4] calling forth in the worshipper attitudes of awe, reverence, and devotion, baffling and dethroning the pretensions of human wisdom. Yet mystery is not the same as mystification. Too much of the latter is excused and acquiesced in under guise of preserving the divine mystery. Mystification easily turns into uncertainty and unfaith, and from this stage it is but a step to the surrender of all that is vital in Christian experience.

We shall not pretend in this book that we have found all the answers. Yet as a minimum the issues can be defined; the biblical faith which bears upon them can be stated; the relevance of this

---

[3] H. H. Farmer, *The World and God* (New York and London: Harper and Brothers, 1936), p. 8.

[4] A mystery which both elicites fear (awe) and attracts to devotion. The phrase was introduced into modern theological diction from Rudolf Otto's *The Idea of the Holy.* He regarded this as the primary attribute of deity, inducing in man a sense of "the numinous," or reverence before the mystery of the divine nature, which is basic to religion.

faith both to the scientific presuppositions of the modern world and to life within it can be suggested. There is no probability that the author's answers to the nest of questions will be accepted by all Christians. Differences of opinion may prove helpful in getting at better answers, provided discussion is carried on with fairness, frankness, and Christian love. It is one thing to "be children, tossed to and fro and carried about with every wind of doctrine"; it is another as mature Christians to differ with sincerity and steadfast faith on matters of great importance. In any case what is presented here is written with the hope that God may find a way to use it "for the equipment of the saints, for the work of ministry, for building up the body of Christ, until we all attain to the unity of the faith and of the knowledge of the Son of God" (Eph. 4:12).

Chapter One

WHAT IS PROVIDENCE?

SINCE THE CENTRAL THEME OF THIS BOOK IS GOD'S PROVIDENTIAL care, it is appropriate to begin with an examination of what we mean by providence. Much discussion gets off base, and those who discuss talk at cross purposes, through lack of any clear understanding or agreement as to what is being talked about. At the same time it must be recognized that one's view of providence is in a measure implied in one's definition of it.

I shall begin by defining the term as broadly as possible and then try to sharpen its meaning from the standpoint of biblical faith and Christian experience. Also, to note what providence *is not* will help to make clear what it is.

1. Some definitions

The providence of God means the goodness of God and His guiding, sustaining care. Belief in providence in the most general sense implies the goodness as well as the power of God in the creation, ordering, and maintaining of His world, embracing the entire world of physical nature, biological life, and human persons. However, it is in the destinies of human individuals that belief in providence centers. Both a positive Christian faith in providence and the perplexities connected with it find their focus in God's care of the individual person.

The word providence is derived from the Latin pro and videre, "to see ahead." By an interesting juxtaposition of English usage it means also "to look after." In a word, to believe in divine providence is to believe that God sees the way before us and looks after us as we seek to walk in it.

It immediately becomes apparent that faith in divine providence, if it is held with any consistency, necessitates faith in a personal God. Only a personal God can know or care what happens to persons. A deity conceived to be an impersonal force or process, or an abstract principle, or the totality of all that exists, or the sum total of human ideals cannot be personally concerned with individuals or their destiny. Such a God may be worshipped in the sense of being held in reverence; to such a deity some form of human adjustment can be made. But such a God cannot be prayed to or trusted to give providential guidance to any person's life. So basic to the reality of providence is the nature of God that we shall presently devote two chapters to this theme.

A personal God is one of supreme intelligence, supreme goodness, and supreme creative and controlling power. One who grants the presence of an infinitely complex, yet ordered, structure in the universe and the predominance of value over evil in human existence may be ready to affirm the existence of a personal God upon these grounds. Yet this is not foundation enough for a doctrine of providence. The Christian's faith in providence requires a further and to many minds a more difficult affirmation, for it roots in the conviction that the God who guides the stars and atoms in their courses also guides and cares for you and me.

It is at this point that many persons today fail to find any meaning or persuasiveness in the traditional Christian doctrine of providence and have found no substitute for it. Included in this number are thoughtful Christians who have surrendered this faith with great regret. From their point of view to say that a personal God is the Creator and Controller of the orderly structure of the world is one thing; to say that this same God has a personal concern for every individual is quite another, with the second affirmation not deducible from the first.

Various factors contribute to this rejection of, or at least hesitancy before, the belief in providence. Doubtless the most basic is the age-long fact of suffering, striking erratically and seemingly unrelated to any benign controlling purpose. To this must be added what seems to many the absence of any convincing positive evidence of providential care, joined with skepticism at the over-facile claims of such evidences frequently made by trusting souls. So closely linked is providence with prayer that the lack of any personal experience of communication with or response from God is another barrier. To one who attempts to view everything from a scientific frame of reference, providence implies miracle and miracle is *prima facie* ruled out as unscientific.

A reason for doubting God's personal and providential care which I have heard frequently adduced is the vastness of the universe and the relative insignificance of each individual human life. In modern terminology one hears stated a replica of the mood of the author of the eighth psalm:

> When I look at thy heavens, the work of thy fingers,
> the moon and the stars which thou hast established;
> what is man that thou are mindful of him,
> and the son of man that thou dost care for him?
> (Ps. 8:3-4)

This ancient mood is reinforced by each new discovery that the universe is far more vast and more intricate than could possibly be guessed by simply looking up at the moon and the stars, and man's conquests of space, though this may call forth admiration for human prowess, brings God no nearer. Even more potent, doubtless, than such considerations is the complexity and the whirling, disconcerting tempo of modern life, with corresponding insecurities of personal life and fortunes. Many centuries ago Aristophanes wrote, "Whirl is king, having driven out Zeus," and this is the state with reference to providence in which many find themselves today.

These are serious considerations, and there is no helpfulness in decrying them. Nor will argument alone, with the presentation of rationally consistent grounds for belief in providence, suffice. For example the sense of smallness before the vastness of the universe is no logical barrier to belief in God's personal care

19

for each individual human soul, for God by His very nature is infinite in wisdom, power, and love, and we finite persons ought not anthropomorphically to place upon Him our human limitations. Yet this may be admitted, and still doubts remain. Only when one feels the love of God does His infinity bring Him near us instead of setting up a further barrier to His personal and providential care.

Disbelief in divine providence or doubts about it may be rooted primarily in either reason or emotion but usually the two converge. In some minds the quest for a reasoned philosophy has led to atheism or to some type of impersonal theism. God's personal care for the individual then seems to have no rational foundation, and to continue the practice of prayer or the attitude of trust in the goodness of God becomes a mockery. For other persons the initial obstacle is not intellectual but personal. A faith formerly held becomes shattered through some dislocation in human relations, or one simply fails ever to find a vital faith amid the entanglements and rival claims of the modern world. Our "sensate culture" seems much more real than God, and belief in the divine goodness becomes so shadowy and evanescent that it is dismissed as the relic of an earlier and more credulous time when people believed not only in guardian angels but in ghosts and witches.

Because disbelief in providence has this dual rational and emotional foundation, any counteracting of such disbelief must proceed likewise on a twofold foundation. This is what this book will attempt to do, and the attempt is made not merely as a matter of strategy but because the Christian faith itself has this twofold nature. The Christian faith means, on the one hand, a body of beliefs—affirmations about the nature of God, of Jesus Christ, of the Holy Spirit, and other pertinent issues of Christian theology which are believed to be true. Christian faith means also personal commitment in loyalty and trust to the God of our faith who has come to us in Jesus Christ and who, in daily companionship through the Holy Spirit, is a nourishing, undergirding power for living. Belief in providence in the Christian sense requires both kinds of faith and requires them in the closest possible co-ordination and mutual support.

The reader is invited to explore this problem with the author from the standpoint of Christian faith. A too naïve faith opens the way to all sorts of vagaries, false hopes, and then crushing disappointment. A too exclusively rationalistic faith shuts out too much and is apt to slam the door shut upon the warmth and vitality of the inner room where the soul meets God. Yet Christian faith does not need to be either naïve or overrational-istic; it can be both reasoned and vital.

In considering providence, therefore, we take our stance without apology on biblical faith and Christian experience. This is not to rule out anything that bears upon the issue from other angles. We shall not disparage any who seek to make their inquiry from the standpoint of empirical observation, hoping thus for a greater objectivity with fewer presuppositions. But let none suppose that by proceeding from some other angle than that of Christian faith he has gained full objectivity or eliminated presuppositions! Experience ought to be observed from all angles, and no faith is well supported in disregard of its evidence. Yet experience is always *interpreted* experience; it never "comes raw" or in complete objectivity. Rejection or acceptance of belief in providence, as in the very existence of God, will always depend in no small part upon the presuppositions from which the given facts of experience are interpreted.

I said a moment ago "biblical faith." The revelation of God's ways with men, reflected in the history of the Hebrew people, coming to clear and supreme expression in Jesus Christ and witnessed to with joyous fervor in the early days of the Christian Church, is recorded for us in the Bible. This rightly stands as the fountainhead of Christian theology, and when flexibility in biblical interpretation is provided for, there can be no disagreement as to its primacy for faith as both truth and life. Yet the Bible is not the only source of Christian truth. There is a great deal in the structure of the universe as a whole and of human life in particular which is relevant to a Christian doctrine of

21

providence, and to the extent that there are factors which seem to negate the Christian's faith, these must be looked at for what they are and not bypassed. We shall in this book draw no sharp line between biblical and natural theology, for it is the author's conviction that since both are channels toward the truth about God and His world, there can be no basic conflict between them. Nevertheless, our primary point of departure for discussing providence will be the source from which the doctrine springs, namely, biblical faith and its validation in Christian experience.

2. Biblical foundations

The meaning of providence, we noted, centers in God's guiding, sustaining, loving care for each individual human soul. That God is "our Father" not only collectively but individually is central to the thought of Jesus and in general to the outlook of the New Testament. Though it is less central to the Old Testament, where the main emphasis is upon God's relation to the nation, it is there implied many times and is particularly evident in the devotional poetry of the Psalms. In spite of repeated questionings and attack—for ours is not the first skeptical era in Christian history—it has been resolutely held to through the centuries. This is more than accidental, for Christian redemption centers in God's relation to the individual, and on any other basis prayer becomes chiefly self-fortification or autosuggestion.

No one needs to be told that this is a day of deep anxiety. This is apparent both in much of our literature and drama which are set in a dark mood and in the attempts of radio and television, the movies and the press to induce more cheerful feelings. The frequency of psychic disorders and of physical troubles mentally induced bears witness to our uneasiness, and the need of inner reassurance is reflected in sermons as in psychiatry. Even today the firmest ground to stand on comes from the Bible, for the Bible reflects the perennial moods of the human spirit and God's answer to them. Speaking of our finitude and of current images in art, poetry, and philosophy of the "abyss," Roger Hazelton remarks, "It comes with something of a surprise to discover that

22

the Bible employs similar tokens of anxiety—the desolate pit, the miry bog, the flying arrow, the deep waters, the shadowed valley, and many others." [1]

It will be impossible to canvass here in detail the biblical foundations for belief in God's providential care. Indeed, when this is conceived as God's care for His chosen people as well as for the individual, it is coterminous with the central theme of the Bible—God's never-failing grace. I shall indicate only a few of the more significant passages.

One of the most basic of these appears in the Sermon on the Mount, as recorded in Matt. 6:25-34. After making due allowance for the fact that the Gospel accounts reflect the thought and experience of the early Church as well as the words of Jesus, it remains true that the authenticity of this passage is almost never challenged. It is an immortal plea on the part of Jesus for trust in God's providential care. Note that in urging his hearers and followers not to be anxious "about your life, what you shall eat or what you shall drink, nor about your body, what you shall put on," he does not say that these matters are unimportant. Indeed, their high importance is attested by the words, ". . . your heavenly Father knows that you need them all." Nor does Jesus counsel laziness and inertia about them. Though activity is not explicitly mentioned in this passage, the "be not anxious" which is its central note is not at variance with diligent effort. Nor does such calm trust in God preclude forethought. At this point the passage needs to be read in conjunction with Luke 14:25-33, in which Jesus gives clear approval to "counting the cost," whether in building a tower, going to war, or becoming his disciple.

Still within the Sermon on the Mount is Jesus' great injunction to prayer in confidence of the goodness of the Father (Matt. 7:7-11). The loving concern of God, infinitely greater than the evident helpfulness of any earthly parent, is the ground of our asking, our expectancy, and our obligation of helpfulness to one another.

[1] *God's Way With Man* (New York and Nashville: Abingdon Press, 1956), p. 25.

Whatever may have happened physically in the incident of the calming of the storm—and of this we shall say more when we reach the chapter on miracles—it is apparent that its central meaning lies in the calming of the storm of fear in the souls of the disciples (Matt. 8:23-27). In the question, "Why are you afraid, O men of little faith?" Jesus affirms the providential care of God as clearly as in any statement in the indicative mood.

A passage often questioned, and sometimes even treated facetiously, is that in which Jesus is reported as saying:

Are not two sparrows sold for a penny? And not one of them will fall to the ground without your Father's will. But even the hairs of your head are all numbered. (*Matt. 10:29-30.*)

It is only the literalist or the person who fails to read the context in which these words are set who need have trouble with them. Jesus was dealing with terribly serious business. He was sending out the Twelve upon their mission in a hostile world, "as sheep in the midst of wolves." So precarious was the situation that they might not return. In this setting he enjoins them, "And do not fear those who kill the body but cannot kill the soul; rather fear him who can destroy both soul and body in hell." Then with a bold hyperbole—a lightness of touch which is not incongruous with the seriousness of the situation but alleviates the tension of it—he speaks these words about the sparrows and the hairs of their head. "Fear not, therefore; you are of more value than many sparrows." That clinches the point! This is one of the few passages in which Jesus speaks directly and comparatively of the supreme value to God of persons, though he everywhere assumes it. To read this passage in the mood of argument as to whether God keeps a ledger recording dead sparrows and hair follicles is totally to vitiate its meaning.

In the setting in which these words are recorded in Luke there follows the further assurance that under persecution and arrest, the disciples need not be anxious about their mode of defense.

24

And when they bring you before the synagogues and the rulers and the authorities, do not be anxious how or what you are to answer or what you are to say; for the Holy Spirit will teach you in that very hour what you ought to say. (*Luke 12:11-12.*)

It is important to note that Jesus nowhere promises immunity from such persecution and arrest. In fact he repeatedly warns his disciples to expect it. Apparently his conception of God's providential care, which should be ours, was not that God would forestall all painful events and prevent their occurrence. Rather, it was that with the Holy Spirit as guide and guardian one need not be anxious in the midst of them.

Some of the most comforting, inspiring words of all literature, repeated times without number in the presence of grief or danger or other forms of pain, are those of the fourteenth chapter of John. It is not necessary to repeat them here in full, so familiar are they, but it may be pointed out that they epitomize a Christian doctrine of providence. Whether or not one can frame it in words of his own or can defend it in argument, one believes in providence when meaningfully he hears the voice of God speaking through the words:

Peace I leave with you; my peace I give to you; not as the world gives do I give to you. Let not your hearts be troubled, neither let them be afraid. (*John 14:27.*)

Faith not only in God's redeeming grace but in His providential care undergirds everything in the letters of Paul. To select one passage among many in which this is implied or affirmed, let us look at Phil. 4:4-7. Probably this was Paul's last message before his death; in any case it was written from imprisonment in Rome with his earthly future extremely precarious. Yet with a paean of confidence he is able to say:

Rejoice in the Lord always; again I will say, Rejoice. Let all men know your forbearance. The Lord is at hand. Have no anxiety about anything, but in everything by prayer and supplication with thanksgiving let your requests be made known to God. And the peace of God, which passes all understanding, will keep your hearts and your minds in Christ Jesus.

Again and again the New Testament writers echo this buoyant and triumphant note. One more only will be cited, selected because it emphasizes the reality of suffering as well as the need of calm reliance on God.

Humble yourself therefore under the mighty hand of God, that in due time he may exalt you. Cast all your anxieties on him, for he cares about you. Be sober, be watchful. Your adversary the devil prowls around like a roaring lion, seeking some one to devour. Resist him, firm in your faith, knowing that the same experience of suffering is required of your brotherhood throughout the world. And after you have suffered a little while, the God of all grace, who has called you to his eternal glory in Christ, will himself restore, establish, and strengthen you. To him be the dominion for ever and ever. Amen. (*I Pet. 5:6-11.*)

It is apparent from even a casual reading of such passages as these, though it cannot be too strongly stressed in view of frequent misconceptions, that the biblical point of view never identifies the guiding hand of God with immunity from pain or deliverance from all danger. There is, to be sure, in the Old Testament a strong emphasis on the rewards of obedience to the God of the covenant, such rewards taking the form of long life, victory over enemies, prestige in the eyes of the people, and even economic benefit. These rewards of virtue are in the New Testament subordinate to the peace and joy that are promised even in the midst of danger and pain. Yet even in the Old Testament God's providential care is most evident at the point where outer blessings are denied.

The Old Testament writers knew well enough the kind of spiritual enemies that assail us today, though they could not foresee the number or complexity of the sources of malaise that were to beset mankind. Yet they knew man must die, and it is when we "walk through the valley of the shadow of death" that we are to fear no evil, for the rod and staff of the Shepherd of men's souls will be near to comfort and sustain us. It is not by accident that the twenty-third psalm is, next to the Lord's Prayer, the most familiar portion of the Bible, for it states in deathless words a doctrine of providence.

The psalmist knew also what it was to stumble and fall in one's spiritual journey and even to be bogged down in envy of those with greater prestige and prosperity. Such words as these describe the state of mind of many today:

> But as for me, my feet had almost stumbled,
>   my steps had well nigh slipped.
> For I was envious of the arrogant,
>   when I saw the prosperity of the wicked.
>   (Ps. 73:2-3)

Happy are we if in this plight we can also say:

> Thou dost guide me with thy counsel,
>   and afterward thou wilt receive me to glory.
> Whom have I in heaven but thee?
>   And there is nothing upon earth that I desire besides thee.
> My flesh and my heart may fail,
>   but God is the strength of my heart and my portion forever.
>   (Ps. 73:24-26)

Enough has been said to indicate that one cannot eliminate the belief in God's providential concern and care for the individual without eliminating with it much that is central to the Bible. But what does providence mean in today's experience?

3. Providence as experienced

There has arisen in recent years a phenomenon which has been referred to as "juke-box religion." In sentimental lyrics our young people warble to each other about "The Man Upstairs" and declare their faith not in the words of the Apostle's Creed but in a modern "I Believe." One of these, entitled simply "He," may be quoted as a sample of them all:

27

HE can turn the tides and calm the angry sea.
HE alone decides who writes a symphony.
HE lights every star that makes our darkness bright.
HE keeps watch all through each long and lonely night.
He still finds the time to hear a child's first prayer.
Saint or sinner call and always find Him there.
Though it makes Him sad to see the way we live,
He'll always say "I FORGIVE." [2]

Two judgments, each to some extent legitimate, can be passed upon such warblings. One is that they are banal, and those who sing them have, in most cases, little understanding of what is being chirruped about. The other judgment is that those who compose and sing these songs, lacking any better way in which to express their faith in providence, are seeking to declare it. This at least must be observed, that such songs would not find favor at all among a sophisticated and unpious generation unless they stirred some emotions at least incipiently religious. Instead of either decrying such expressions or accepting them as the equivalent of Christian hymnody, it is better to see them as marks of an incipient faith in providence and a yearning for more.

Turning now to a different range of maturity, what does providence mean today to a deeply dedicated Christian? In particular what does it mean to a mature person who, in time of trouble, feels sure beyond a doubt of God's guiding and providential care? To answer, I shall let one speak for herself. The letter which is quoted here was not written with any thought of defending a doctrine of providence but comes so white-hot out of life that I filed it under this heading when it came to me. A Korea missionary, caught at the outbreak of the war before the advancing Communist hosts and obliged to flee in haste from Seoul with the entire mission, wrote on June 29, 1950 to her family and friends at home this account of their experiences:

Each started with one suitcase, and some water, crackers, etc. Our dear Korean cooks had set bread at 2 A.M., so we had hot loaves to

[2] Words by Richard Mullan, *He* (New York: Avas Music Publishing Co., Inc., 1954).

start with. Mattresses from cots lined the bottom and sides of the open trucks, our station wagon and four jeeps started out loaded. Voelkels station wagon wouldn't start, but "Old Faithful," our 1946 Ford, made the trip all the way over terrible roads and high passes to Taejon—arrived there 6:30 P.M. There were 80 of us. We got a quick supper at the Army Mess and put the children on mattresses on the floor as we heard we could get a train to Pusan in the morning. A Mr. Emmons connected with the State Department was in Taejon and told us he'd been sent to prepare a place for President and Madam Rhee, but when he'd phoned back, the situation in Seoul was so improved the President was remaining in Seoul. Ned returned from the R. R. Station after 11:00 and at 11:30, Ned and I stretched out on the floor of Margie's living room (over protest but others needed the beds more) and at midnight we were called to "leave immediately by vehicles" as the Communist troops landed on the East Coast were driving toward Taegu and it would be a race past there. Actually when we reached Taegu we went up to the Mission Compound for an hour and a quick meal under the trees there.

Tuesday, we drove hard and fast, from 1 A.M. till about 7:30. Then Old Faithful couldn't make it further and our load was jammed into other conveyances—Ned and I each being sixth passenger in a jeep. The suitcases were abandoned in Taejon[3] but we had each carried some juices and raincoat or whatever we selected. Tuesday's drive was most grueling but God's Hand was on us all the way—has been marvelous. Aunt Fan's truck given to the Orchards Project carried thirty-five, children and women mostly, to safety—George did a marvelous driving job. Once over a bridge so broken we emptied the truck and he rushed it across to our prayers and cheers. A long night detour had probably Providentially saved the truck-load of children from going through another bridge where a smaller army baggage truck (last three of Army personnel and baggage out of Taejon) had gone through just ahead of us—we were able to ford the stream. Drought made dozens of streams passable. Flats by the score were repaired and repumped—all vehicles have taken a terrific beating. The Army jeep we arrived in at Taegu came in on the rim of one

---

[3] The writer has since supplemented the account with this significant observation, "When we were told to discard our suitcases, the three things I grabbed from mine were (1) my Bible, (2) my toothbrush, (3) my raincoat—in that order."

wheel within a mile of the city, and a Taegu chauffeur came out for us just before our party took a train (a "special") for the two-hour ride to Pusan. The goodbye to Ned and the rest in the rain there was not easy, but again we trust His leading.

No one has heard from the five Methodist missionaries "caught" in Songdo. Southern Presbyterians had not reached Pusan yet by Tuesday night. Must stop now—we're being moved out of the barracks to a rest camp somewhere. Love, Sue.[4]

Note that at the time this was written there was no fore-knowledge of how things might turn out, either for those whose perilous exit is here described, the husband Ned who chose to stay behind to look after those suffering and imperiled in Korea, or the five Methodist missionaries caught in Songdo. Eventually, though in the historic case of the latter not until after many months of stringent captivity, all came through to safety. But does God's providential leading lie *only* in such deliverance? There is no suggestion in this letter that trust in God's leading would stand or fall with a particular outcome. Had dire disaster befallen all, as did happen in the case of the eleven missionaries massacred in the Philippines during the second world war or the five who were slain by the Aucas in Ecuador in 1956,[5] those who loved them could still believe by the light of Christian faith that God had not forsaken them.

4. Providence and predestination

But must we believe that God predestines all circumstances to happen as they do? It cannot be too strongly affirmed that *providence does not mean predestination.* It is at this point that much confusion centers, and many who think they cannot believe in providence are in reality rejecting belief in predestination. The Christian cause is not well served by assuming that whatever

[4] Used by permission of the writer, Mrs. Edward Adams.
[5] For a stirring testimony to faith in providence even though fidelity in witness should lead to death, see the account written by Elisabeth Elliot, the widow of one of these men, in *Through Gates of Splendor.*

happens is God's will. The implicit logic of such an assumption is, "Whatever is, is right." Neither biblical faith nor Christian experience substantiates this conclusion. Indeed, to talk either about the conquest of sin through the grace of God or the call of God to alleviate preventable suffering would be meaningless if God ordains and is pleased with every circumstance in the lives of His human children.

To revert for a moment to the letter above quoted, can we say that God predestined and approved the Communist invasion which precipitated these events? or the break-down of the Old Faithful station wagon? or the broken bridges? or the flat tires? Hardly! Though for different reasons, both communists and Christians must reject this assumption. The hand of providence appears in the conquest of these difficulties, not in their occasioning. Though the writer of the letter is not attempting here to offer fine points of analysis, her spiritual insight is sound in ascribing to God's purpose the overcoming of these obstacles, not their occurrence.

There will be more to say about this distinction when we look at the various types of forces involved in the shaping of human destiny. For the present let it be understood that one may believe in providence as the guiding, protective, loving care of God without believing that God predestines every event to happen as it does.

Predestination, as it has been held in the history of the Church and is still held by a diminishing number of Christians, has two related but not identical meanings. It can mean foreordination to redemption by the grace of God in Christ, that is, a doctrine of divine election. This is what it apparently means in Rom. 8:29, 30 on which a doctrine of predestination to salvation is chiefly based. But predestination may also be taken to mean that God foreordains every particular event. On this view no matter what happens among the manifold details of life, God wills it, and therefore, it is to be accepted with resignation.

It is predestination in this second sense that we are here concerned with. Paul apparently believed in predestination in

31

the first sense, though it is probable that his words in Rom. 8, so long the basis of a doctrine of divine selectivity, were prompted by his overwhelming conviction of our inadequacy to save ourselves from sin and hence the need of utter dependence on divine grace. But it is virtually certain that Paul was not a predestinarian in reference to every event of everyday living. Had he been so, his constant moral injunctions to the churches to change their ways would have had no point.

Paul believed powerfully in providence, and his words on this subject, just before and after the passage above referred to, still sustain us with their great resounding affirmation of confidence in the goodness of God.

We know that in everything God works for good with those who love him. . . . If God is for us, who is against us? He who did not spare his own Son but gave him up for us all, will he not also give us all things with him? . . . Who shall separate us from the love of Christ? Shall tribulation, or distress, or persecution, or famine, or nakedness, or peril, or sword? . . . No, in all these things we are more than conquerors through him who loved us." (Rom. 8:28, 31, 35, 37.)

Nobody has ever said it better! But Paul never says that everything that happens is just the way it should be.

Providence means the guiding hand, the encompassing goodness, the supporting power of God in any situation, however dark, however evil, however unwilled by Him. If God guides, then He has a plan, a "best good," a destiny toward which He seeks to lead us. We may thwart it, and others may thwart it. Faith in providence centers in the confidence that however much His will may be thwarted, God never forsakes us—God never "lets us down."

5. General or special?

Before concluding this chapter a distinction needs to be drawn between what is often called the "general providence" of God and "special providences." General providence means the goodness of God as seen in the overall, inclusive structure of creation.

To the philosopher it means that this is a purposeful universe, that there are axiological or value structures so inherent in the very nature of existence that no naturalistic explanation, but only a personal God, is sufficient to account for them. What may thus be stated and argued in formal language is expressed by the "man on the street" in the simple judgment, "It's a good old world!" or in "juke-box religion" by such words as these:

I believe for every drop of rain that falls, a flower grows;
I believe that somewhere in the darkest night a candle glows . . .[6]

What is basic to a Christian doctrine of general providence is expressed with great beauty and dignity in the refrain of the Genesis story of creation, "And God saw that it was good." This is echoed in the familiar words of Jesus about the heavenly Father who feeds the birds of the air and clothes the grass of the field.

For reasons previously suggested, belief in general providence is less often disputed than a belief in special providences. Unless one is disposed, on the one hand, to doubt that God has anything to do with the structure of the universe, or on the other to reject all natural theology and hence all natural grace, the way is open for faith in the essential goodness of creation. The way, though open, is not self-evident in view of the world's evil. For this reason we must know what we mean by the Christian doctrine of creation and how it is related to the nature of the God on whom our world and our lives depend. This will be the principal theme of the third chapter.

The term "special providences" is much more ambiguous. It may mean events thought to happen outside the regular course of nature by the supernatural power of God, that is, miracles. It may mean that God does for one person what He ordinarily does not do for others in the form of special favors or some special protection, and it is then usually linked with specific answers to prayer. Or it may mean luminous events of special significance

---

[6] Drake, Shirl, Stillman, & Graham, "I Believe" (New York: Cromwell Music Company, Inc.).

in which, with extraordinary clarity, we see the hand of God leading, guiding, and sustaining us. Sometimes without clear differentiation it has all three of these meanings. A person who believes that in answer to prayer he has been miraculously saved from danger or healed of some serious illness, and thereby directed by God into new channels of life, might regard his experience as a special providence in all these senses. Yet it does not necessarily presuppose them all. The basic factor that makes a special providence to be so considered is that an individual should believe he sees the hand of God within particular events, guiding and sustaining him in time of need and leading him toward some particular God-given destiny.

The position that will be defended in this book is that special providences occur, but that they take place within, not in isolation from or in contradiction to, a structure of general providence. This is in effect to say that there is no need to rule out miracles and special answers to prayer, but there is large need to know what we mean by these terms and how they fit into a larger whole.

It would be a tempting enterprise to move directly into this question. However, more spadework must be done. We have said that providence does not mean predestination. Yet destiny is a very closely related concept. To see what is involved in destiny in general may help us to see more clearly the meaning and implications of providence in particular. Not only must we note more precisely the differences between providence and predestination but also between providence and an idea much more common in current thought—namely, that of an indifferent and impersonal fate. This will be our task in the next chapter.

Then, when these distinctions are before us, we must undertake a study that will be basic to any satisfactory answers to the problem of evil or to the affirmation of providence. What is the nature of God? And how is He related to our world? These queries lie at the very heart of Christian concern. Without knowing what a Christian may believe about the God who creates and redeems us and how His sovereignty is related to our human freedom, any answers to particular problems must be tentative and premature.

So it will be several chapters yet before any specific attempt is made to define prayer and miracle or to answer the particular questions that impinge on our day-by-day trust in God's providential care. Yet if the reader will be patient, we shall come to them in due course! Groundwork must be done and foundations laid.

Chapter Two

PROVIDENCE, DESTINY, AND FATE

ONE OF THE PERENNIAL HANDICAPS UNDER WHICH ONE WORKS IN any theological writing is that everything one can say presupposes something else. And it is not possible to talk about everything at once! Yet it is the close-knit relation of everything to God that makes theology what it is and provides its perpetual challenge.

The previous chapter indicated the meaning of providence, both in biblical faith and in Christian experience, and suggested the existence of special providences within a wider structure of God's general providence. It was categorically affirmed that providence does *not* mean divine predestination of every detail of human existence, lest such an identification disregard the existence of evil in all its stubborn reality and justify an unwarranted assumption that whatever is, is right. Yet the difference between providence and predestination is so crucial that further exposition is called for. Furthermore, though providence ought not to be identified with predestination, this does not rule out a close relationship to destiny. To examine this relation will be the main function of this chapter.

In the shaping of human destiny how are God's will and man's will related? Is everything determined by God? Then we have a doctrine of predestination which, if carried to its logical conclusion, would leave ground neither for human freedom nor moral responsibility. Is nothing determined by God? Then we have several alternatives. There is naturalism, tracing all events and man's supposedly free decisions to physical and biological forces, social pressures, and social conditioning. Or there is

36

humanism, allowing some place for human freedom and moral ideals, and hence for responsible choice, but none for God's providential care. Or there is the nihilistic type of existentialism which asks no metaphysical questions because it believes no meaningful answers are to be found, but in denying the meaning of life asserts an atheistic metaphysic of its own of which the keynote is an impersonal fate. Or one may hold to a mixture of naturalism, humanism, and nihilism with no clear distinction among them.

Whatever defense may be given theoretically to any of these positions, Christian faith and life recoil in practice from all of them. The Christian feels as if he could make some responsible choices; otherwise, a sense of guilt, which he is bound to have at least occasionally, would be meaningless. Furthermore, his faith compels him to assert that life does have some meaning—a meaning which he does not devise by his own subjective wishful thinking or find created by the society around him but a meaning given by a Determiner of Destiny. What this meaning is he may but dimly grasp; but that there is a meaning to be found and a power beyond man's feeble effort that sustains him in the quest for it is what keeps him from surrendering to humanism or nihilism.

Man is a free agent but never wholly free; God determines human destiny but never arbitrarily. But how are both sides of this paradox to be held together?

This is our problem. We shall begin once more with some definitions of terms, then look to see what there is in the idea of destiny that may throw light on a Christian doctrine of providence.

1. What is destiny?

Destiny is not an easy term to define. In popular usage it connotes whatever lies ahead of a human individual or group and is bound to happen. The word itself does not indicate whether this future is inevitably fixed or somewhat variable; much less does it say whether such fixity as there is is due to natural, human, or divine causation. Nevertheless, to talk about destiny at all is to imply something personal, something projected toward the future, and something patterned rather than inchoate and haphazard.

Such qualities of destiny are implicit in common usage. One speaks of the course of the stars, the life history of a plant or animal, of the present orbit and probable future of the satellites in space, but not of the destiny of any of these. Looking backward, we examine our heritage and trace the course of previous experience, but it is in looking toward the future that we speculate upon or seek to discern our destiny. And even though much in the past or present may seem so meaningless as to fit into no pattern, to predict even the unpredictability of life is to affirm a kind of destiny.

These qualities of destiny center in the fact that it is intensely personal. It is the expression of selfhood in interplay with that which lies beyond the self, indeed, in relation to the widest possible context of the self. At this point the intuition of the common man which leads him to ask, "Who am I? What lies ahead of me?" is reinforced by the wisdom of the philosopher. Says Paul Tillich:

Our destiny is that out of which our decisions arise; it is the indefinitely broad basis of our centered selfhood; it is the concreteness of our being which makes all our decisions our decisions . . . Destiny is not a strange power which determines what shall happen to me. It is my self as given, formed by nature, history, and myself.[1]

To say that destiny is personal and centers in our selfhood is not to deny its collective character. There are destinies of families and of nations as well as of individuals, and one of the moot problems today, in view of the possibilities of global annihilation, is the destiny of the human race. Nor is "myself as given" to be conceived wholly as "formed by nature, history and myself," for

[1] *Systematic Theology*, I 184-85. Copyright 1951 by the University of Chicago.

providence means that myself as I now am and as I shall be in the future depends in some significant manner upon the activity of God in nature and history. Nevertheless, the centrality of the personal for the understanding of destiny is basic to its nature and will be presupposed in all that follows.

Several characteristics of destiny are important to our understanding of it and through it to an understanding of providence. The first of these is that as one looks toward the future, considering his destiny, he never can predict it with accuracy. He walks toward the future with a confident faith or with a deep apprehension, yet he walks toward the unknown. The poet Whittier caught this mood perfectly, giving expression to the goodness of God in relation to human lack of foreknowledge, when he wrote:

> I know not what the future hath
> Of marvel or surprise,
> Assured alone that life and death
> His mercy underlies.
>
> . . . .
>
> I know not where His islands lift
> Their fronded palms in air;
> I only know I cannot drift
> Beyond His love and care.[2]

Here is faith in providence, not at variance with the fact that even with our best calculation of probable events, we still "know in part." The reverse of this is found in the dark forebodings, anxiety, and tension that beset the life of the person whose outlook toward the future lacks any ground of confident trust.

The future, as one looks toward it, is seldom a completely blank wall. As surely as we know that wholesome food will nourish our bodies and potassium cyanide will poison them, we know as rational beings that some things will lead to satisfying results and others will not, and it is the part of a mature morality

[2] John G. Whittier, The Eternal Goodness.

to make the best possible calculation of the probable future. Yet both from lack of human wisdom and from the infinite complexity of our world, some things will always remain uncertain. Much depends upon how we adjust ourselves to this uncertainty.

A second characteristic of destiny is that acceptance of it or recoil from it significantly determines one's decisions, choices, loyalties, and meanings in the present. The person who carries a rabbit's foot for good luck or for his protection a medal that has been blessed at a shrine, the soldier who thinks that he will live until the bullet "with his number on it" hits him, the bereaved person who accepts his loss with fortitude because "it was to be," the Christian who can say with Paul, "We know that in everything God works for good with those who love him,"—all are believers in destiny, though on various levels, and all respond to situations differently than they would without this belief. There is a kind of comfort and power to endure that is generated by any of these grounds of confidence though some supports, based on false or flimsy foundations, can too readily turn into cynicism and despair. Only the faith that is based on a true understanding of God and His relation to the world will hold under intense or long-continued strain.

A third characteristic of destiny is that, however inevitable it may be thought to be, it is never accepted in experience as eliminating all freedom of choice or human effort. One may carry a fetish or talisman for luck, but one still jumps out of the way of an approaching automobile if he can! One may believe that the time of one's death is already fixed, but the sane man tries to avoid it by sensible precautions. Even at the highest levels of God-centered faith one prays, "My Father, if it be possible, let this cup pass from me," (Matt. 26:39). The completion of this prayer in "nevertheless, not as I will, but as thou wilt," may well be regarded, as it usually is by Christians, as the highest form of prayer. Yet this acceptance of God's will and providential control is voluntary, not coerced, acceptance. To suppose that Jesus went to the cross without any volition on his part is to destroy at its roots the meaning of his self-giving in love for our redemption.

This interplay of freedom with necessity has particular importance with relation to the question of human sin. Those types of Christian thought which have been most predestinarian have never cancelled freedom to the point of being willing to condone sin and thus assume a completely fixed destiny. This appears very clearly in the thought of John Calvin. Writing of the Spiritual Libertines of his time, whose pantheistic tendencies he thought made them believe everything to be the work of God, he says:

> In so doing they attribute to man no free will, any more than if he were a stone; and they remove all distinctions between good and evil so that nothing can be done wrongly, in their opinion, since God is the author of it. . . . Example: Some one has committed adultery? One cannot chide him for it; for that would be to blaspheme God. A man covets his neighbor's wife? Let him enjoy her if he can; for he would only be doing the will of God, and even that would be a divine act.

The consequences of this view were to Calvin utterly loathsome. With his characteristic precision he enumerates them.

> Three dreadful consequences follow. The first is that there would be no difference between God and the devil—indeed, the god they forge for us is an idol worse than a devil in hell. The second is, that men would no longer have any conscience to avoid evil, but like brutes would follow their sensual appetites without discretion. The third is, that everything would have to be adjudged good—whether adultery, murder or theft—and all the crimes imaginable could be regarded as praiseworthy acts.[3]

What Calvin could not see was that his own predestinarian view, if carried to its full logical conclusion, would come out at the same spot. If everything that happens is foreordained and

---

[3] From *Contre la Secte des Libertins, Calvini Opera*, VII, 183.

predetermined by an agency beyond human control, then either sin is nonexistent or it is God's fault and not man's. Since this is a conclusion no Christian can accept, something must be wrong with the premises.

A similar inconsistency is found in psychological determinism. This is at the opposite pole from a Christian doctrine of predestination, both in reference to divine control and human sin, but it has a strange affinity with it in attempting to deny human freedom. It is the view that biological inheritance, social conditioning, and past experience so set the grooves of a person's thinking and acting that his apparent freedom of will is an illusion, and all is determined by forces he cannot control. With the object of making all human action a part of nature and thus subject to scientific prediction and control, this view has been widely advocated by many psychologists, sociologists, and other social scientists. Though it has its usefulness in helping to trace the sources of human behavior and is particularly useful in accounting for abnormal behavior, this position has two very serious limitations: (1) it assumes without evidence and in contradiction to Christian faith that man simply is a part of nature, and (2) in denying freedom of choice, it has no logical place for moral responsibility. It leaves each man subject to a kind of inexorable fate; yet the holders of this view often appeal, as illogically as Calvin, to moral incentives. Proponents of this position characteristically defend it, not on the basis that they themselves are so conditioned that they have no choice in the matter, but that by processes of free and rational decision they have adopted it as right and true and worthy of support.

Therefore, it appears that this attempt to limit man's freedom, like the predestinarian, bogs down in inconsistency. Furthermore, while this type of determinism posits a kind of fate in terms of the inevitable consequences of prior conditions, it has no real sense of destiny, for to disregard man's freedom is to make him a complex form of animal or machine which has no historical future or moral destiny.

Destiny, then, looks toward the future but never with full

foreknowledge of it; what one believes about the future significantly affects one's living and acting in the present; any attempt to deny man's freedom to affect his destiny ends by bringing back through the window what was put out at the door. What have these facts regarding destiny in general to do with a Christian doctrine of providence? This must be our next inquiry.

2. Inferences regarding providence

Destiny, we have said, always envisages an unknown, or at least a partially unknown, future. This is important to a doctrine of providence, for providence never means simple prediction. To believe in providence is to believe that one not only can but must "walk by faith, not by sight," (II Cor. 5:7). If it were possible to calculate the human future with the accuracy and precision with which astronomers and mathematicians can predict an eclipse of the sun or moon, it is doubtful that anyone would talk about trusting in providence. It is at the point of one's faith, hope, and loyalty to God in spite of the hazards of an unknown future that the idea of providence takes on a meaning that no mere calculation of future events could possibly have.

Furthermore, it is wholly legitimate to see best the workings of providence *after* events have transpired rather than predicting them in advance. To assume to know exactly how or where God will lead us involves not only arrogance and human presumption but is too often tinged with wishful thinking. One wants a certain vocational opportunity to come his way or an escape from some unpleasant situation to open up or the unraveling of a family tangle to take place. To say that one *knows* it will happen is from one point of view an act of faith, but a faith too often ending in shattered hopes when the human will attempts to dictate to God what He must do. The deeper and more Christian kind of faith is that which faces the future unafraid, awaiting in serenity of spirit what the unfolding days may bring, and thanking God as a pattern of good emerges even in the midst of darkness.

It is often charged by the skeptical that Christians are prone to interpret as special providences what are merely coincidences, since it is only in retrospect that such providences are discovered. An apparently chance meeting becomes the basis of an acquaintance that leads to a marriage or a new job or some other life-changing development, and afterward one says, "It was the hand of providence." Since at the time the original contact occurred one would not think of calling it by this name, there is the suspicion that the only providential element is what one reads into it in retrospect. Is this suspicion justified?

It is true that the same event may be regarded, according to one's point of view, as coincidental or providential. The admission of this fact does not, as some fear, necessitate the surrender of the reality of providence, for there are reasons for this situation. The first is that providence like prayer, miracle, and, indeed, faith in God in its totality is a religious category. It is meaningful only to the religious person; to another it is something simply to speculate about if not to scoff at. There is nothing in human existence that may not be termed coincidence rather than providence if one starts from presuppositions which lead him to favor this point of view.

Furthermore, even the deeply religious person may need to exercise some caution as to saying precisely what events are providential. There are occasions, such as narrow escapes and remarkable deliverances from danger, wherein it does not lie within human wisdom to say why one person should be saved and another should perish. Hence, a due amount of reticence is in order. Yet it is never inappropriate to see God at work in anything that seems right and good. Nor is it appropriate to limit providence to what can be seen as providential at the moment when crucial events occur. It is of the very nature of the Christian's faith in providence that human wisdom cannot predict its course in advance and often fails to see its full significance in the present, but in looking backward can discern a pattern that makes it seem appropriate to say, "Thus far the Lord has led me on."

A second characteristic of destiny, we saw, is that what is be-

44

lieved about it makes a profound difference in the present. From one point of view this is simply to state the obvious fact that ideas, whether true or false, make a difference in emotional attitudes and reactions to situations. It is not necessary to accept a pragmatic or instrumentalist [4] view of truth to recognize that what one believes affects greatly the way he lives and what he does. One who thinks he is sick—and thinks this long and hard enough—gets sick; one who believes he is getting well convalesces far better than one who does not. This simple fact is at the root of much faith healing, both of body and mind, and underlies the current cult of reassurance through holding positive and confident thoughts.

The question that emerges inevitably is this: "Does providence exist only in the mind of the person who believes in it?" In other words is it his faith, and not any objective ground of faith, that gives him support? If so, then Christianity rests on a vast illusion, for it is imbedded in Christianity that God is real and that God guides, guards, and supports those who put their trust in Him.

To revert to some of the examples cited in the previous section, it is not true that a rabbit's foot, a bit of metal blessed by a priest, or even a New Testament carried over one's heart will ward off gunfire. There is no impersonal fate, written either in the stars or in mysterious "numbers," that determines the issues of life and death, though there are so many contributory factors within God's world that when we do not understand them, we are likely to say "fate" to cover lack of knowledge. We ought not to begrudge any comfort to be found on a fictitious basis. But neither ought we to be content with it either for ourselves or others. To seek protection on the basis of a charm, even when the fetish is a religious object, is not to ensure a "charmed life" but to court the disillusionment that magic often brings. To trust in fate gives no real support, and one is equally likely to shrink from the outcome when the time of testing comes.

---

[4] Instrumentalism as a type of philosophy denies that there is any absolute truth but regards all relative truth as defined by the way in which ideas work to promote better human adjustment.

To trust in providence is to trust in the goodness of God, whatever happens. It does not involve belief that everything that happens will be to our liking. It does not even involve belief that everything that happens is exactly as God would have it, for it is in the very nature of evil to be at variance with God's will. To trust in providence is to believe that however dark or evil a situation may be, God is with us, and with the help of God good can come out of it.

Such trust is important from two angles; first, what one considers providential, and second, what God is actually able to do with and through those who trust Him.

Providence, like revelation, is a two-sided matter. What God endeavors to disclose man must appropriate, or there is no disclosure. Similarly, when God leads through human events toward the fulfillment of His will, man must seek to follow, or there is no leading. Without such human response of will and spirit, the idea of providence fades out to be replaced by explanations in terms of coincidence, natural forces, or an inexorable fate. This is not different in principle from the fact that when a person doubts or denies that God reveals Himself, revelation for him ceases to exist. God may indeed be seeking to disclose Himself or to lead us without our awareness, but without faith we do not accept this disclosure as revelatory or this leading as providential.

Faith is essential also from the standpoint of what God can actually do in human lives. Jesus made it clear that faith was a requisite to the doing of his "mighty works," and this is as true in the twentieth century as the first. God enables the man of faith to face both the major crises and "life's minor collisions" with courage, calm, and a sense of direction. Without faith life is a mixture in varying proportions of happiness and discontent. The faith that is the precondition of "the peace that passes understanding" cannot be merely a subjective feeling. Faith to the Christian is faith in the actual goodness of God, not a bogus, whistling-in-a-graveyard optimism. This is why we must presently examine carefully the grounds of believing not only that God exists but that the God who creates and redeems is good.

46

We shall later devote a chapter to the relations of providence to prayer, and it is therefore not necessary to say everything here that bears upon this important subject. A word must be said, however, on the relations of faith to prayer for the occurrence or the non-occurrence of particular events in the shaping of human destiny. Shall we upon setting out on a journey pray for safety or upon launching a new enterprise pray for its success? By all means if the journey or the enterprise are believed to be in accord with the will of God. Shall we pray for the health or the well-being of our loved ones? It would be either a very skeptical or a self-centered Christian who did not. But there are two things we must not do. We ought not to insist that God must give us what we desire. His will and purpose may be, and very often is, quite different from ours. And second, we must not disregard the physical and social forces in the midst of which God shapes our destiny. Some things are possible; some are not in the kind of world God has given us, and to demand the impossible is not to show faith in Him but to assert our own self-will.

A third note in destiny was found to be the persistence with which human freedom reasserts itself even in theories that try to eliminate it. This too has its bearing on a Christian doctrine of providence.

It is essential to affirm at the same time man's freedom and the limitations upon his freedom. Every sane, mature person is free enough to make responsible moral choices which gravely affect his life and destiny; yet nobody is wholly free. No one could, in a true sense, be a person unless he were able to make moral choices, though in infancy or unconsciousness or in abnormal psychic health his selfhood is not abrogated by temporary interruptions of his freedom. It is this capacity for responsible moral decision that primarily marks the difference between the human spirit and all forms of subhuman animal life. Such moral choices gravely influence one's future destiny and one's response to the leading of divine providence. Yet it is equally true that in making these choices one is limited by the conditions of his body, by his time and place and in general by his physical and social environment, by his degree of maturity, by his own past choices, and by the total natural order established by God in creation. This can readily be admitted without accepting all the postulates of a deterministic psychology.

Every man's freedom is limited by the very fact that he is finite—that he is man, not God. "To err is human," and every man errs at times in his judgment as to what he ought to do. Still more tragically he fails in his power to do the right and falls into sins of overt commission and of moral dullness and lethargy. Though the present writer does not hold to the view often put forward today as biblical theology—that *every thought and act* is sinful (and does not believe that Jesus held this view)—it is certainly true that every person who has reached the age of responsible choice misuses his freedom and thus sins. Then sin fastens chains about him, and until he is freed as a forgiven sinner by the grace of God, his freedom becomes more and more constricted.

It is not only individual sin but the complexities of human social relations that entangle us. In part it is the sheer complexity, unpredictability, and unmanageability of these relations that restrict our freedom; in part it is social sin—the defiance by groups, as well as individuals, of the will of God. There are "orders of creation," of which the primary ones are the family, economic life, and the political institutions of society, which we may believe ordained of God and established within His good purpose for mankind. But this is far from saying that whatever happens within these orders is God's will! Nothing is more evident than that sin and selfishness, to say nothing of human frailty and error, corrupt them all. "God setteth the solitary in families," (Ps. 68:6, K.J.V.), but He is not responsible for family bickering and quarreling and broken homes. God gives us work to do and the resources of the earth to nourish us but not the exploitation, the drudgery, and the irresponsible use of power that so often infect economic life. That there should be ruling powers and governing authorities is apparently the divine will, but this does not justify acquiescence in tyranny under the

48

assumption, "For there is no power but of God: the powers that be are ordained of God." (Rom. 13:1, K.J.V.).

Every man's life is set within the framework of these and other converging social orders. We do not live in an ideal world wherein only our own recalcitrance is a barrier to the doing of God's will; we live in an actual world of restricting physical and natural forces and of very complex social relations.

All this may be admitted without surrender of faith in the overarching providence of God. In fact the assertion both of our freedom and of the limitations upon it is basic to any true understanding of God's ways with men. To deny the reality of human freedom is to cut the ground from underneath moral responsibility and thus encourage the notion of an inexorable fate. To disregard the limitations on our freedom is to court disaster as one attempts to do what he cannot do, or expects to have what he cannot have, and then sinks into a morass of cynicism, frustration, and despair. Neither way is the way of Christian faith.

3. Fate and fatalism

It has been necessary in discussing destiny to make some references to fate, since this is one kind of belief in destiny. Yet it has qualities of its own which distinguish it from both predestination and providence, and which set it apart from that understanding of destiny which can be constructively related to providence.

Fate connotes impersonality. What happens simply happens. When the question is raised as to why it happens, the fatalist has no answer, and he covers his lack of explanation by saying that "fate" caused it. This, we must repeat, is not simply the reticence of the Christian who hesitates to claim more knowledge than he has. There is a legitimate and necessary muteness before the mystery of God's ways that prompted Job, after the Voice had spoken from the whirlwind, to say reverently:

> Behold, I am of small account; what shall I answer thee?
> I lay my hand on my mouth.
>
> (Job 40:4)

Job, though he had found no rational explanation of the mystery of evil, had been brought to a deeper dependence and a clearer vision of God until he could also say:

> I had heard of thee by the hearing of the ear,
> but now my eye sees thee.
>
> (Job 42:5)

The view of the fatalist is no such reverent submission before the personal will of an all-wise God; it is, on the contrary, a declaration of forced submission to a vague impersonal "something."

This impersonal something that is called fate is somewhat variously conceived. From one angle it goes off into astrology, crystal gazing, palmistry, or other forms of fortunetelling. In popular thought, as has been noted, it is the bullet that has one's number on it that will take off the hapless soldier and nothing can be done about it, though illogically he may carry a good luck charm that his sweetheart gave him on departure. The person engaged in ordinary, less hazardous enterprises is affirming a kind of fate that he thinks pursues him when things do not go according to his wishes, and he cries out in dismay, "That's just my luck!" Possibly also, though less probably, he may affirm a more cheerful fate by exclaiming, "I must live right! Things always come my way!"

As has already been observed, this quasi-magical, illogically grounded idea of fate may at times give some psychological support. It may even be partially identified with a predestinarian view of destiny, for the person who holds that whatever happens occurs because "it was to be" or that one dies "when his time comes" often fails to distinguish whether he thinks God or something else causes this event. However, insofar as events are attributed to fate rather than to God, the idea is impersonal, hence, nonprovidential.

In some historic, non-Christian conceptions of fate there are semireligious overtones. In Greek tragedy, where destiny is a more dominant note than in any literature outside of Christian thought, the nemesis in store for the evildoer caught in the toils of his own choices casts a dark and fateful shadow upon the human scene; yet it is also a kind of impersonal divine judgment to teach men their rightful ways. In the early Greek myth of the three Fates who determine human destiny—Clotho who spins the skein of life, Lachesis who measures it out, and Atropos who cuts it—there is an approach to personal determination by deity. Yet in Greek mythology the gods themselves are subject to the decrees of fate, and it remains an essentially impersonal concept.

In Hinduism the law of Karma, an important part of Hindu religion as well as culture, is still more impersonal. Centering in the belief that one's present choices and acts will determine future incarnations, it has the reflexive influence of making one's present the product of the past and thus breeding a sense of futility that cuts the nerve of effort. In spite of the great minds and souls that India has produced, no one can have much contact with popular Hinduism today without sensing the apathy and hence the obstruction to social progress that this type of fatalism encourages.

Fate, as an affirmation of the ultimate meaninglessness of existence and the powerlessness of man before it, holds no small place in the thought of the West today and its literary expressions. Man's despair at his inability to master circumstances and control his destiny, which Paul Tillich calls man's "estrangement," is often conceived by the determinist as an encompassing, impersonal fate. Says Tillich in a succinct description:

Estrangement as fact has been explained in deterministic terms: physically, by a mechanistic determinism; biologically, by theories of the decadence of the biological power of life; psychologically, as the compulsory force of the unconscious; sociologically, as the result of class domination; culturally, as the lack of educational adjustment. None of these explanations accounts for the feeling of personal responsibility that man has for his acts in the state of estrangement. But each of these theories contributes to an understanding of the element of destiny in the human predicament.[5]

[5] *Op. cit.*, II, 56-57.

From one point of view this variety of proposed explanations is simply a restatement of the constricting forces limiting man's freedom, which were noted in the previous section. But what makes this a deterministic view of fate is the substitution of a set of causal factors for purpose. Teleology is rejected. The determinist of this stamp finds no evidence of guiding purpose—much less of a controlling providence—but he does find evidence that man's actions and reactions are causally connected. To some degree, and often with striking clarity, these sequences can be traced. To trace them is the delineation of a fate in which there is no ultimate source or goal and no purpose beyond what man, perchance, in his helplessness can inject into an otherwise totally meaningless existence.

As a consistent determinism this point of view holds less place in philosophical writing than it did a generation ago. The rise of psychotherapy based on the depth psychology, though it has not proved God, has tended to disturb the mechanistic explanation of man's spirit. "Psychotherapy is one version of modern psychology which cannot get along without the 'psyche.' It sees physical, biological and unconscious processes as participating in the life of a self which is held together, in the end, by consciousness and purposiveness." [6]

Yet in much popular thought and writing this recognition of man's freedom has wound even more tightly the coils of an impersonal fate. Man is free to get himself into a mess and to drag others along with him, and a dark shadow hangs over all.[7] This is the dominant note of the atheistic existentialism of our time, whether in its philosophical or literary expressions.[8]

It lies outside the scope of this book to comment at length upon this type of existentialism. However, the vogue not only of Jean-Paul Sartre but of such Pulitzer and Nobel Prize winners as

[6] David E. Roberts, *Psychotheraphy and a Christian View of Man* (New York: Charles Scribner, Sons, 1950), p. 95.

[7] Note the similarity, though on very different foundations, between this view and Augustine's *posse peccare*, man's freedom to sin but not to save himself.

[8] There are also types of theological existentialism which are not atheistic and are not under discussion here.

Eugene O'Neill, Tennessee Williams, and Albert Camus cannot be overlooked. Even the titles of their works are suggestive of a dark fatality. Sartre's *No Exit*, O'Neill's *The Ice-man Cometh* and *A Long Day's Journey into Night*, and Camus' *The Myth of Sisyphus*,[9] with its portrayal of man's endless frustration and the futility of all human endeavor, may be taken as illustrative. The plays of Tennessee Williams, most of which have been phenomenal box-office successes, are not simply pictures of human sordiness and sensuality, as they are sometimes assumed to be, but of an engulfing fate that keeps man from being anything else but sordid and sensual.

The persons who write such plays and novels are men of consummate literary skill. Yet even this would not account for the wide vogue of such writing were there not a deeper reason. It is because so many people believe life to be meaningless and the hope set forth by Christian faith to be illusory that such writers "speak to their condition." There are moments of humor and of brightness and pleasure in such writing, as in life, but for the most part the impression left is that fate condemns man to suffering and sordiness in a meaningless world.

I shall not reply specifically to this point of view, for this entire book is an attempt to reply to it. No elaboration is needed to make it evident that the atheistic existentialism of our time is completely at variance with the Christian idea of providence. Such a portrayal of human existence may have value in puncturing overoptimistic illusions and shattering the complacency of the too comfortable; it cannot build faith or hope. The egocentricity of the human heart may be vividly portrayed, as it is by Camus in *The Fall*; this does not of itself induce a Christian sense of repentance for sin and acceptance of the divine mercy. If existentialism of this type is right in its assumption, then providence is nonexistent. The reader may choose.

[9] It will be recalled that Sisyphus in Greek mythology was condemned always to roll a stone to a top of a mountain, only to see it slip from his hands and roll down again just as he reached the summit.

4. Some conclusions

To return to the main theme of this chapter, destiny when viewed in connection with providence is always personal, and in this sense existential, but it is the product of God's and man's activity together. This is to affirm that destiny is both a divine gift and a human enterprise wrought out in the midst of manifold forces and conditions. To "achieve one's true destiny" means that there is for every individual not only a future but a best future that God stands ready to help him discover and pursue.

One ought to find the divine plan for his life and bend every energy toward its fulfillment. Yet "circumstances alter cases," and these circumstances constantly shift through choices made by oneself and others, and through the force of impinging natural events. For example, when one becomes blind, it is no longer his duty or destiny to pilot an airplane; the violinist who loses an arm may have to find some other way to release the music in his soul. Having married one woman, a man cannot marry another while she lives.[10] Such restrictions do not mean that God no longer has a chosen destiny for the person involved. They mean, rather, that God's continuing purpose and goal may need to be sought, found, and followed under new structures of life and experience.

If what has been said thus far is true, God has for no man a fixed and final destiny in the sense of either an inexorable fate or an assured state of outward security. There is no escalator carrying us steadily upward, or downward either. Life under the best circumstances remains hazardous, yet even under the worst it can be undefeated, and there is nothing in all creation that can separate us from the love of God and His guiding care. One who believes in such a fluid yet controlled and sublimely adventurous destiny believes also in providence.

We must move now into a very crucial area—an examination of the nature of God and of His relation to His world. Many

[10] This is not to deny the legitimacy of divorce under some circumstances. The illustration is chosen because marriage is, or ought to be, one of the most crucially determining factors in human life.

assumptions, indeed, we have already been obliged to make as to the nature of the God of Christian faith in order to discuss providence at all. But in view of the persistent reality of evil it is not enough to make assumptions without examining implications.

In the three chapters which follow we shall be dealing with the problem of evil, but not with evil as an isolated problem. Rather, we shall try to speak affirmatively of what can be believed as to the creating, redemptive, sovereign power of God. Through this positive approach, rather than through a theodicy which starts with evil and then attempts to justify the ways of God to men, we shall hope to arrive at a firmer faith in the Eternal Goodness.

Chapter Three

THE GOD WHO CREATES

IN ANY SATISFACTORY ANSWERS ARE TO BE GIVEN TO THE PROBLEMS
outlined in the previous chapters or helpful suggestions given
from a Christian standpoint to those who find their lives engulfed
in a meaningless existence, it must be from the context of a
Christian understanding of the nature and reality of God. This
is to say that theology is relevant to personal Christian living,
for theology means the study, or the doctrine, or the understanding of God. Christian theology has many facets, but God, as
we find Him through Jesus Christ, is central to them all.

Though the Bible does not use the philosophical term "personal God," its assumption throughout is that God is personal.
The God who not only creates but loves, rebukes, judges, redeems, delivers, guides, guards, and sustains His people; the God
who sorrows for their sins and in mercy offers salvation; the God
who is the basis of the Christian's faith and hope and love is
meaningless unless conceived in personal terms. The Bible does
not argue this position; it assumes it, for the Bible is not written
as speculative philosophy but as the record of living religion. On
this assumption the entire structure of the great drama of creation, judgment, and redemption rests.

It should be clear that to say, "God is personal," is not the
same as to say, "God is human." The problem of anthropomor-
phism—the conceiving of God in human terms, the making of
God in man's own image—is a serious question for many minds
and has driven not a few into the ranks of the humanists or
theistic naturalists. Yet these substitutes, whereby one thinks of
God as simply the human urge toward value and goodness or as

an impersonal process at work in man and the universe, do not solve the problem. They are prone to fall into such a vagueness and inconsistency that for lack of concreteness and coherence they fail to meet the demands of clear thinking, and by denying the personal nature of God, they suck the marrow out of the structure of belief on which personal Christian experience is formed. The Christian who reads the Bible carefully and honestly will not hesitate to admit that at some points, particularly in the Old Testament, God is represented in terms that are "human, all too human." According to Gen. 3:9 God had a conversational encounter with Adam while walking in the garden in the cool of the day, and doubtless many persons have been puzzled, as I was when I learned the Ten Commandments as a child, over the words, "For I the Lord thy God am a jealous God." Nevertheless, in spite of incidents and passages wherein God is represented not only as jealous but cruel and even bloodthirsty,[1] and in spite of strong emphasis throughout much of the history of Christian thought on the "wrath" of God, the biblical representation of the nature of God as holy, righteous, merciful, and loving is amazingly free from crudely anthropomorphic traits.

In the Bible God is the Lord of all the earth who is Creator, Judge, Redeemer, and Father. These terms and the ideas they stand for are found in the Bible again and again. To these may be added a fifth, not in biblical diction but implied throughout, the Lord of history. The Lord who has made the heavens and the earth with man as His supreme creation is implicated in the destinies of men and cares what happens both to nations and to individuals. It is obvious that this is very closely related to a doctrine of divine providence.

In the next chapter we must give primary attention to those aspects of the nature of God which center in His righteous love and redemptive concern for persons. However, as was pointed

---

[1] The clearest examples are in the patriotic poetry and in some of the psalms. (Cf. Jud. 5:23-27; Ps. 52:5; 60:6-8; 79:5-7; 80:4-6; Nah. 1:2; 2:13-3:7.) Such passages represent the indentification of the people's emotions with those of their deity, and therefore, the imputing to Him of their own attitudes.

out in the introductory chapter, the crux of the problem of belief in the Eternal Goodness for the modern mind is how to think of such loving divine concern in connection with the apparently impersonal structures of nature. We turn, therefore, to examine our Christian belief in God the Creator.

1. Creation in the New Testament

The usual procedure in examining the biblical view of creation is to begin with the Old Testament and most frequently with the first two chapters. We shall reverse this process, for what is most central to Christianity is found in the revelation of God in Jesus Christ. Those who recognize that the New Testament is our starting point, as do Emil Brunner in *The Christian Doctrine of Creation and Redemption* and Edwin G. Lewis in *A Philosophy of the Christian Revelation*,[2] commonly find their index to the meaning of creation in the prologue to the Gospel of John or in other passages which suggest that Jesus Christ as the Creative Word was God's agent in creation. There is great meaning, which we shall examine presently, in such statements as, "In the beginning was the Word, and the Word was with God, and the Word was God. He was in the beginning with God; all things were made through him, and without him was not anything made that was made." (John 1:1-3.) However, in my judgment it is in the recorded words of Jesus that we find our clearest evidence of the nature and meaning of creation, and from these we get light to understand better the more cryptic passages.

a) *Jesus' view of creation.* In the words of Jesus we find no full-blown doctrine of creation. Jesus, we must remember, was not a speculative thinker or systematic theologian; he was a person sent from God who lived in such intimate fellowship with God that when we read his words and behold his deeds, we ourselves are drawn to God in worship and service. What Jesus assumed about God and reflected in his total ministry we may

---

[2] Brunner, op. cit., pp. 6-9; Lewis, op. cit., pp. 92-101.

safely assume to be the truth about God's nature and God's relation to men.

Throughout the Gospels we find Jesus speaking and acting from the conviction that this is our Father's world. In some places this is explicit, as in the Sermon on the Mount where he speaks of the Father's making his sun to rise on the evil and the good and sending rain on the just and the unjust (Matt. 5:45). He assures those who are unduly anxious about food and clothing that the Father who feeds the birds, adorns the lilies, and makes the grass to grow will surely provide for their needs also (Matt. 6:25-33). In an arresting figure of speech he asserts that the Father who cannot be unconcerned about the falling to earth of one of his sparrows will surely be more concerned about men who are of much greater value (Matt. 10:29-31). The institution of marriage, according to Jesus, is based upon the fact that "from the beginning of creation God made them male and female"; therefore, the two that God has joined together, man must not put asunder (Mark 10:6-9). Besides such explicit references to God's creation of and rulership over the earth, Jesus' constant use of parables drawn from the common things of nature is indicative of the fact that to him God's world and God's truth were in close connection.

Such familiar passages do not answer all our questions. Yet they indicate something of great importance. This is that *in the outlook of Jesus there was no cleavage between creation and providence. The same God who made the world can be trusted to provide for His children within it.* It is bedrock for Christian faith and something to be included in any elaboration of Christian doctrine.

b) *Christ as God's agent in creation.* The union of God's creative handiwork with his providential care in the outlook of Jesus gives a clue for interpreting other more difficult New Testament passages which seem to center the creation in Christ himself. In addition to the words in the first chapter of John which were previously quoted we find such statements as these:

He is the image of the invisible God, the first-born of all creation; for in him all things were created, in heaven and on earth, visible and invisible, whether thrones or dominions or principalities or authorities —all things were created through him and for him. He is before all things, and in him all things hold together.[3] (*Col. 1:15-17.*)

In many and various ways God spoke of old to our fathers by the prophets; but in these last days he has spoken to us by a Son, whom he appointed the heir of all things, through whom also he created the world. He reflects the glory of God and bears the very stamp of his nature, upholding the universe by his word of power. (*Heb. 1:1-3.*)

These passages, like John 1:1-3, declare that God created the world through Jesus Christ. To these may be added others which do not mention creation specifically but either in words about Christ or in words attributed to him in the fourth Gospel state that God had a purpose in him "from the foundation of the world."

Blessed be the God and Father of our Lord Jesus Christ, who has blessed us in Christ with every spiritual blessing in the heavenly places, even as he chose us in him before the foundation of the world, that we should be holy and blameless before him. (*Eph. 1:3-4.*)

He was destined before the foundation of the world but was made manifest at the end of the times for your sake. (*I Pet. 1:20.*)

Father, I desire that they also, whom thou hast given me, may be with me where I am, to behold my glory which thou hast given me in thy love for me before the foundation of the world. (*John 17:24.*)

Jesus said to them, "Truly, truly, I say to you, before Abraham was, I am." (*John 8:58.*)

Such passages have given rise to the Logos doctrine of creation. According to this view Jesus Christ existed "before the founda-

---

[3] See also Paul's statement in similar vein in I Cor. 8:5, 6.

tion of the world"; through him all things were made; in him all things maintain existence, or as the statement in Colossians graphically puts it, "in him all things hold together." God the Father is still the Creator, but it is through His Son that creation has taken place. The Logos, called "the Word" from the beginning of John's Gospel and also "the Son" from the relation of Jesus Christ to the Father, is the second person of the Trinity.

This Logos view of creation through the pre-existent Christ has been widely held by Christians through the centuries and is stated in majestic language in the Nicene Creed, repeated in countless services of worship. After affirming belief in God the Father Almighty, Maker of heaven and earth and of all things visible and invisible, it continues:

> And in one Lord, Jesus Christ,
> The only-begotten Son of God;
> Begotten of his Father before all worlds,
> God of God,
> Light of Light,
> Very God of very God;
> Begotten, not made;
> Being of one substance with the Father;
> By whom all things were made:
> Who for us men and for our salvation
> Came down from heaven,
> And was incarnate
> By the Holy Ghost
> Of the Virgin Mary,
> And was made man.

There is no need here to trace the complicated Christological controversies of the early Church which gave rise to this statement. Its meaning today is probably more often *felt* than understood, and those who cannot feel its great overtones are apt to recoil from it as an archiac bit of verbiage. Our purpose here is not to defend or reject it but to try to make clear what truth it indicates.

Can we believe today in a pre-existent Christ "by whom all things were made"? In one sense, no; in another, possibly; in another, yes. It depends on what we mean by the pre-existent Christ.

The most obvious meaning, which many people connect with it only to reject the whole idea, is that Jesus lived before Jesus lived. As a human being born of Mary in Bethlehem and dying on a cross in Jerusalem approximately thirty-three years later, his biological existence is clearly limited to that particular era in history of which we have the record in the New Testament. Any other assumption does violence not only to common sense but to the basic Christian conviction of an historical incarnation within the conditions of human life.

The second possible meaning is of a pre-existent soul, waiting to come to earth in a human body at such a time as God might ordain. This is consistent with the Platonic idea of the pre-existence of souls before birth, and something like this, with reference to the souls of all persons, is reflected in Wordsworth's "Ode on the Intimations of Immortality." Christian faith has not generally held such pre-existence to be true of all persons, and it is an idea much more consistent with Greek than with Hebraic thought. However, it is not an impossible concept. The personality of Jesus Christ, as the unique Son of God, need not be limited to what applies to other persons, and his pre-existence as eternal Spirit need not be ruled out as unthinkable.

However, this does not seem the most helpful way to deal with the Logos doctrine. To center attention on the existence of Jesus Christ as an individual person "before the foundation of the world" is apt to obscure the greater meaning implied in the passages where this phrase is found. There the emphasis is placed on God's eternal plan and purpose which was brought to fulfillment in him. The key to understanding both the biblical and the Nicene statements is found *in the union of creation with redemption in the nature and purpose of God.*

It is no accident that in the Nicene statement, "By whom all things were made," is followed immediately by, "Who for us men and for our salvation came down from heaven." Similarly in the prologue of John, "without him was not anything made that was made" is linked inseparable with the next words, "In him was life, and the life was the light of men." (John 1:3, 4). In the other passages cited, the context indicates that it is not creation alone or redemption alone that is being proclaimed but the good news of both made vital and life-transforming through Jesus Christ.

If we take this union of creation with redemption as our index, we do not need to say that Jesus as God's incarnate Son lived pre-existently or created the world, though he still retains his rightful place in Trinitarian thought as God's supreme revelation and our redeeming Lord and Savior. What we can say is that the eternal divinity that became incarnate and was manifest in him— the divinity that makes us call him "Christ" and not simply "Jesus"—has no beginning and no end. In this divinity, creation and redemption meet.

It is "God the Father Almighty"—the loving Father Jesus showed Him to be, the almighty Sovereign of the created universe—who is "Maker of heaven and earth." The world did not simply drift into existence; it was made by a purpose and plan. It is the same God that made the world, who through Christ redeems the world. It is the same God with the same loving, long purposes who both creates and saves us. This divine purpose before the incarnation took the form of the long-anticipated work of Jesus Christ for men. In the fullness of time it came to historical fulfillment in Jesus Christ. It is known to us today through Jesus Christ as eternal goodness in union with creative power.

This leads to a very important conclusion, both about providence and about the Logos. The Logos in nature—the rationality, purpose, and design it manifests—speaks to us of the wisdom and power of God on a grand scale. The Logos in Christ finds its fullest meaning in God's redemptive love for persons. Yet the Logos in nature and the Logos in Christ are not two but one. The Creative Word is also the Redemptive Word, waiting to bring to fulfillment through Christ both God's eternal purpose for mankind and God's particular purpose of good for the life of every man. On this foundation providence is assured.

2. Creation in the Old Testament

We turn now to look at the Old Testament, where on the whole the issues are simpler if one grasps the appropriate frame of reference from which to interpret what is found. The Old Testament view of God's creative action is based (1) on the creation stories of the first two chapters of Genesis and (2) on references to the majesty and power of God found in many passages, and particularly in the nature poetry. While these sources in their deeper meaning are largely in agreement, it will be helpful to look at each separately.

a) *The creation stories.* As every student of the literary structure of the Bible knows, Gen. 1 and 2 contain two creation stories—Gen. 1:1 through 2:4a being from the "P" document, Gen. 2:4b to the end of the chapter from "J." Dates are difficult to assign with any exactness, but it is certain that "P" is postexilic and probably from the fifth century B.C., while "J" is among the earliest writing in the Bible and is to be dated somewhere between 950 and 850 B.C. Thus, the first story is relatively late in its origin, the second early, though both were doubtless long carried down in the oral tradition before being put into writing.

Relative dates, however, become inconsequential when set over against another very crucial fact. This is that *both narratives are completely prescientific.* Science, as we use the term or even as Aristotle used it, had not been dreamed of in Hebrew thought. It was not the purpose of either author to give a scientific account of the way in which creation took place. Had they set out to be scientific, even the most naïve common sense would have prevented placing the creation of vegetation on the third day before the sun on the fourth! The purpose of these great prose poems, of which the account in chapter one has a singular beauty and majesty, is wholly religious. It is some unknown seer's way of paying his own and his people's tribute to God as the source of all that is.

Accordingly one of the greatest disservices ever done to an intelligent Christian faith, setting up barriers which have turned great numbers of people away from the Bible and the Church and hence from Christ, has been the literalizing of these stories. In an earlier day, when there was no body of scientific evidence as a basis of comparison, belief in a six-day creation in the manner here recorded did no harm more serious than to carry along a wrong idea which was no special barrier to Christian piety. It still remains true that there are many dedicated Christians among the biblical literalists, though one could wish that differences might be maintained in charity without dissension or bad feeling. When it becomes not the privately held opinion but the unanimous judgment of competent scientists that all the evidence converges to refute the literal accuracy of these stories, then to try to cling to them is to do serious injury to personal Christian faith.

However, to say this is not to say that there is no truth in these stories. There is profound and meaningful truth in them, which must be stanchly maintained by Christians against every naturalistic idea that the world had (or has) no creator and against every allegedly theistic explanation in terms of an impersonal cosmic force or process. It is one thing to say, as Christians well may, that God created and still creates through agelong processes; it is a very different matter to say that the processes are self-caused or self-explanatory or without any ultimate cause, purpose, or explanation. To hold to the latter is to deny what the Bible and Christian faith stand for in regard to the personal, loving creativity and control of God over His world. To attempt, as is sometimes done, to deny creation by a personal God yet keep the fruits of Christian faith in the ethical motivation or even in the redemptive power of Jesus is to surrender the foundation on which the faith of Jesus rested.

It is essential, therefore, to discover the deep and abiding truth that is carried by these stories. Several elements of permanent truth and great value are found in them, and without "proof-texting" one may find great affirmations within the stories that express these insights.

There is, first, the affirmation that *God is the Creator of all that is.* "In the beginning God created the heavens and the earth." (Gen. 1:1.) Science cannot deny that, for it is outside its province; Christian faith must affirm it. Christians may differ as to the meaning of "in the beginning." The most natural reading is probably the truest; that time began with the creation of the world (not our earth planet but the universe) by the eternal God. There is no evidence to contradict it, and the logical difficulties of thinking of time as having a beginning are no greater than to assume its infinity at both ends. Nevertheless, all that "in the beginning" must mean is that God initiated the process by which the world came into being.

The dominant Christian tradition has usually maintained that creation was *ex nihilo* (out of nothing). This has sometimes encountered resistance at the point of the scientific dictum, *ex nihilo nihil fit* (out of nothing, nothing comes). However, all that is essential for *ex nihilo* to mean is that God is not the artificer or fashioner of some previously existing stuff, as the Demiurge in Plato's *Timaeus* introduces order and form into formless matter, but rather that all that exists proceeds from and depends upon God's creative will. God may have always been creating, and there is a suggestion of this in the Spirit of God moving on the face of the waters to bring order out of chaos.[4] Yet if an eternal creation is affirmed, it must still be maintained that it is God who has always been doing the creating.

The truth is that we know nothing at all about the manner of God's initial creative act. We were not there when it happened, and the scientists cannot tell us. What we do know is that God created, and controls, and continues to create an infinitely complex world. About the various natural and biological processes in which His creativity is discerned, science can tell us much.

[4] Gen. 1:2.

What can be learned about God's ways of working through the regularities of nature, we ought gratefully to receive. What we must not do is to confuse ultimate causation with chemical, physical, or biological processes and try to make the latter a substitute for God.

A second truth to be appropriated from the first chapter of Genesis is *the goodness of creation.* This is expressed in the refrain that is repeated at the end of nearly every stanza of this great hymn, "And God saw that it was good." (Gen. 1:10, 12, 18, 21, 25, 31.) James Weldon Johnson in his sermon (in reality a poem) on "Creation" in *God's Trombones* expresses this feeling in moving words second only to the biblical account itself. For example he thus describes the creation of the sun, moon, and stars:

> Then God reached out and took the light in his
>   hands,
> And God rolled the light around in his hands
> Until he made the sun;
> And he set the sun a-blazing in the heavens.
> And the light that was left from making the sun
> God gathered it up in a shining ball
> And flung it against the darkness,
> Spangling the night with moon and stars.
> Then down between
> The darkness and the light
> He hurled the world;
> And God said: That's good! [5]

We shall later have more to say about the problem of evil. Yet all that it is really essential to say on the subject is compressed into the great refrain of the Genesis story. God saw, and we ought to see, that the world is good in spite of the evil that infests it. By the time the "P" writer penned these words, Israel had seen a great deal of suffering—conflict with her enemies, loss

[5] (New York: Viking Press, 7th ed., 1935), p. 17-18.

of nationhood, exile in Babylon, painful return, and precarious rebuilding. Yet it seemed wholly appropriate to this writer that God should rejoice in the goodness of His world.

In our time one ought not lightly and jocularly to declare, "It's a wonderful world!" in the presence of the world's misery. Yet the Christian knows that it is. Jesus wept upon occasion; yet nothing could alter his confidence in the goodness of God and the basic goodness of God's creation. The Hebrew seer who wrote the first chapter of Genesis lived in a society simpler than ours but with no immunity to pain, and his insight into the goodness of God's world is of perennial truth and meaning.

A third great insight is with reference to *the nature of man*. Made in God's own spiritual image, made male and female, man is God's supreme creation. There is a telling answer to every social system that impugns the dignity of man or that belittles the importance of women in the words, "So God created man in his own image, in the image of God he created him; male and female he created them." (Gen. 1:27).

The *imago dei* means that man is created with qualities of mind and spirit that make him truly a person, not a biological organism only or subhuman animal. As God is personal, so is man a person in terms of his capacity for making moral choices, his rational intelligence, his concern for love and goodness, truth and beauty, though always with the limitation that man's personality is derivative and incomplete while only God's is infinite and perfect. The most distinctive attribute of man is his free spirit, whereby he may either sin or seek after God in obedient love, and in this he reflects the image of the eternal.

Creation in the image of God means that all men, and not some fortunate few or some unusually righteous few, are precious to God. It is the final answer to race prejudice, class distinctions, national cleavages, and every other form of man-made separation. Much the same note is conveyed in the New Testament by Jesus' teaching all men to call God, "Our Father"; hence, the recognition that all ought to be regarded and treated as our brothers, children of God, and of inestimable worth to Him. The Hebrew people did not always act upon the principle of the divine image in every man; indeed, they were many times far from acting on it, and the Christian Church has professed more often than practiced the equality connoted by this symbol. Yet here it stands, pointing the way toward human dignity.

Throughout the centuries society has given to men a position of authority and dominance not often granted to women, and neither the Bible nor the Church is free from this disparity. Nevertheless, a very early charter for equality before God, and hence the rightful equality before men, of the female half of the human race is here presented. It is not men only but men and women together who are created as responsible beings bearing the image of God. This, rather than the creation of woman from Adam's rib which appears in the earlier "J" story of Genesis 2, seems to be the true representation of woman's status.

The image of God is, of course, no guarantee against human sinfulness. In fact it is man's nature as a spiritual being, with the freedom that distinguishes him from the animal or the machine, that makes him able to sin—and this he always does. There is significance in the fact that the story of creation is followed immediately by the story of the Fall, and not a little theological controversy through the centuries, which has its echoes in the present, centers in the state of man after the Fall. As the first two chapters of Genesis need not be taken literally, neither should the third; yet there is a great truth there which cannot be disregarded. We shall discuss it later in connection with the God who redeems. It is enough to point out here that reference to the Fall of man through the sin of Adam appears nowhere again throughout the Old Testament, though the story of human sin is on every page.

The point of importance in this connection is that creation remains good in spite of human sin. There is a pessimistic view, formulated first by Marcion and the Gnostics, that the world we know is so bad that it cannot be the work of God the Creator. There is the opposite overoptimistic view that the world is as it should be, with its apparent evil due only to our inability to see with the eyes of God. The more accurate biblical and Christian view is that there is much real evil in the world, both of sin and suffering, from which God seeks to deliver us and against which He calls us to labor in His name; yet creation itself is not evil. Man's capacity to sin designates him as truly human; he has power to triumph over both sin and suffering through the grace of God.

The fourth note of great importance in the creation story is *man's stewardship and delegated responsibility.* It is to men and not to any of the myriads of subhuman creatures that God has said, "Fill the earth and subdue it; and have dominion over the fish of the sea and over the birds of the air and over every living thing that moves upon the earth." (Gen. 1:28). Since these words were written, man's world has enormously expanded, and it is much fuller both of "living things" and inanimate objects than this nameless author could imagine. Yet man's stewardship before God and his responsibility to "have dominion," not in self-exaltation and self-sufficiency but as a God-given trust, remains unchanged. In fact man in his economic life is only beginning to realize the necessity of holding all that he has in stewardship to God. Not until this is more fully realized will the resources of the earth, which God has made abundant enough for all, be so distributed that all men may have enough to satisfy their needs and be able to rear their families in comfort and security.

b) *Elsewhere in the Old Testament.* We must now look more briefly at the references to God as creator in other parts of the Old Testament. No attempt will be made to enumerate them all, though explicit references appear most frequently in the nature poetry of the Psalms, in the messages of the prophets, and in the voice from the whirlwind at the end of Job. The assumption that God is both the creator and the ruler of the world underlies implicitly the covenant relation between Yahweh and His people, the giving and enforcement of His law, and much else that is basic to Hebrew thought. Again we must note what elements of permanent truth are indicated.

In the first place Hebrew thought never separated the rulership of God over nature from His rulership over history. Much more is said about the second than the first; hence, it is customary to think of God's covenant relation with His chosen people, His judgment on their sin, and His promise of a Deliverer in historical terms. Yet the Hebrew mind did not draw the distinction we are too prone to make between God's sovereign control over the physical world and over the destinies of men. Yahweh was the Lord of both, and though men might sinfully flout His holy will, they could not dethrone His power. "Shall not the Judge of all the earth do right?" (Gen. 18:25.) though it appears in an early story of the "J" (Jahvist) document, is implicitly the theme of the entire Old Testament. Its setting in the account of God's threat to destroy the wicked of Sodom and Gomorrah is characteristic of the union of divine judgment with power, though in later thought judgment became much more tempered with mercy. All the way from the early myths of the tower of Babel and the flood to the apex of prophetic preaching in the voice of the Second Isaiah, God's dual control over nature and history is the undercurrent of Hebrew thought.[6] An illustration drawn from the great prophet of the Exile will indicate this:

> Who has measured the waters in the hollow of his
> hand
> and marked off the heavens with a span,
> enclosed the dust of the earth in a measure
> and weighed the mountains in scales
> and the hills in a balance?
> Who has directed the Spirit of the Lord,
> or as his counselor has instructed him?
> Whom did he consult for his enlightenment,
> and who taught him the path of justice,
> and taught him knowledge,

[6] This is not to say that Hebrew thought was uniformly monotheistic. Yet even in its henotheistic stages, when one God was worshiped while others were believed to exist, Yahweh alone had any real power or authority. (Cf. Josh. 24:14, 15; Exod. 15:11; Pss. 95:3, 96:4,5; 135:5-7.)

and showed him the way of understanding?
Behold, the nations are like a drop from a bucket,
and are accounted as the dust on the scales;
behold, he takes up the isles like fine dust.
(Isa. 40:12-15)

A second note is the contrast between God's majesty, holiness, and omnipotence and man's feebleness. The idea of man's having been made in the divine image, though it recurs again in Gen. 5:1 in the genealogy of descent from Adam, is not dominant in the Old Testament. It is man as sinful, weak, and erring within a disobedient nation that is central, and man's dignity appears at the point of God's caring enough for His chosen people, even in this state, to offer forgiveness and deliverance. There are great passages such as "The spirit of man is the lamp of the Lord," (Prov. 20:27.) and the affirmation of the psalmist:

Yet thou hast made him a little less than God,
and dost crown him with glory and honor.
Thou hast given him dominion over the works of thy hands;
thou hast put all things under his feet.
(Ps 8:5-6)

Nevertheless, it must be admitted that a high valuation of man is much more characteristic of New Testament than of Old Testament thought. It appears today more prominently in types of theology which center in the Jesus of the Synoptic Gospels than in those based primarily on prophetic and Pauline concepts of man's sin and weakness.

In the New as well as the Old Testament man is always subordinate to God, not only in goodness but in power. What is impossible for man is possible for God, whether in matters of personal salvation or in the miracle stories that indicate God's power over nature.[7] The meaning and possibility of miracle as scientific fact we must leave for discussion in a later chapter, but

[7] Cf. Matt. 19:23-26; Rom. 8:20, 28, 37; Eph. 3:20.

72

what a miracle connotes in terms of God's power to do what man cannot is basic to the biblical idea of God's creation and control of His world. It is basic also to the instilling of a mood of humility in a day when man is inclined to trust too much his own intelligence and technological skills, or in reverse to fall into a mood of cynicism and despair.

Man's "creatureliness" is a fact which ought never to be forgotten and which ought to be incorporated into any Christian theology. Yet it is not our subordination or our futility alone that needs to be stressed; it is man's dependence on God's gracious and sovereign but never arbitrary power. In the magnificent final chapters of Job, Job is beaten down into silence by the Voice which declares the all-powerful control of God over nature, and there is a suggestion at the end of a personal vision of God that induces repentance.[8] Yet here the main thought is not of grace but of God's incomprehensible omnipotence. For a clear expression of the union of divine grace with the glory of creation we must look elsewhere, and this is again found at its best in the words of Second Isaiah:

> Seek the Lord while he may be found,
>   call upon him while he is near;
> Let the wicked forsake his way,
>   and the unrighteous man his thoughts;
> let him return to the Lord, that he may have mercy on
>   him,
>   and to our God, for he will abundantly pardon.
> For my thoughts are not your thoughts,
>   neither are your ways my ways, says the Lord.
> For as the heavens are higher than the earth,
>   so are my ways higher than your ways
>   and my thoughts than your thoughts.
>
> For as the rain and the snow come down from heaven,
>   and return not thither but water the earth,

---

[8] Job 38:1–42:6, especially 42:5, 6.

> making it bring forth and sprout,
>   giving seed to the sower and bread to the eater,
> so shall my word be that goes forth from my mouth;
>   it shall not return to me empty,
> but it shall accomplish that which I purpose,
>   and prosper in the thing for which I sent it.
>
> (Isa. 55:6-11)

It is doubtful that there is to be found in all literature a more concise and meaningful statement of man's sinfulness, dependence, and creatureliness and of God's mercy, power, and purposeful providence.

The point at which we come out, after this survey of both the New Testament and the Old Testament ideas of creation, is a simple yet very profound one—simple enough for any child to grasp, yet profound enough so that human wisdom can never fully probe its mystery. This is God's world; God made us and loves us, and we can trust Him. The God who creates the world, with all the mixture of good and evil that we find in it, is the same God who redeems and delivers us from evil.

3. The world as we find it

The preceding pages have attempted to set forth the biblical point of view on which Christian faith has been erected and on which, at least in main outlines, this faith has stood through the centuries. But what of the world as we find it? Does this of necessity invalidate the biblical position? On the contrary, at some very vital points it corroborates it.

There is, first, the orderliness and regularity of processes in nature, without which there could be no natural law and no science. To illustrate, there could be no calculation of the simplest falling object, no building of houses on firm foundations, no ships or airplanes, no intercontinental ballistic missiles, no satellites in space unless the law of gravitation were dependable. This force, in conjunction with other well-known laws of mechanics, is basic to our physical existence. How do we know when a full moon or an eclipse of the sun or even the daily rising

74

of the sun will occur? Because these heavenly bodies do not go wandering erratically through space but keep to their established courses. So much do we depend upon these established regularities of nature that ordinarily we do not stop to think about the miracle and marvel of them. An atomic scientist has written:

Other examples of coherence and dependability in nature . . . are the freezing of water at 32° F; the burning of wood, coal and other fuels; the strength of a steel girder; or the regular beating of our hearts or expansion and contraction of our lungs in breathing. Our lives depend on the reliability of great numbers of such processes. The long history of the universe is filled with them and indeed without the coherence and dependability which they provide we would not be able to write its history at all.[9]

There is a greater degree of precision and regularity in the natural sciences such as physics, chemistry, and astronomy than in the life sciences, where individual variations must be reckoned with and scientific description often takes the form of statistical averages. Yet here also there are great regularities of structure and functioning which make possible these sciences. Unless there were discernible cause and effect relations in living cells and tissues, there could be no biology and no dependable physiology, anatomy, or medicine. Even in psychology and the social sciences, where human freedom plays a vital role, there are great common patterns on which our lives are grounded.

In short both the vast ranges of scientific knowledge possessed today and the practical achievements this knowledge makes possible rest upon a bedrock fact—the orderliness and dependability of nature. Long before this great body of knowledge was accumulated, men saw the connection between the orderliness of nature and the the reality of God and spoke of the cosmological argument for God's existence.

[9] William G. Pollard, *Chance and Providence* (New York: Charles Scribner's Sons, 1958), p. 76.

One does not hear as much about the cosmological argument today as formerly, partly because science has so pre-empted current thought that men tend to regard it as having all the answers, partly because theology rests chiefly today on biblical revelation rather than on an examination of nature. Nevertheless, if it is used with proper caution, the cosmological argument has validity.

Science cannot prove God's existence. This lies beyond its province, and science affords no substitute for biblical faith. Neither has science the data to disprove God's existence, as some too dogmatically assume. What science does is to provide a great and ever increasing amount of evidence as to the marvelous intricacy, orderliness, and interacting unity of the universe. It is the legitimate prerogative of religious faith to see in these facts the work of a Creator—a Supreme Mind and Power—who has brought the world into existence and sustains it in ordered unity.

But is this Creative Intelligence good? Though science need not ask this question, it is a vital concern of religion. To this query may be posed another, "Would we want to live in a haphazard, uncalculable, utterly disorderly world of nature?" The answer is obviously no. Upon such order as we have depends much of the security of our living. In spite of the unpredictable elements in human existence, human life has a dependable base without which it probably could not exist, and if it existed would be far more chaotic than it is.

A second factor in the world as we find it is the evidence of purposeful progress and advance. This too gave rise long ago to an argument for the existence of God called the teleological, or the argument from purpose or design. This like the cosmological is often disparaged today, and it should not be overstressed or regarded as fully proving God's existence. Yet used with due restraint, it says something that ought not to be decried.

There are evil and apparently purposeless elements in nature. We may well believe that God requires of men that we work with Him to eliminate them. Yet creation as a whole shows an upward trend, not forward movement at every point, but growth and development. Far from being in opposition to Christian

76

faith, the evidences of evolution indicate direction and control toward purposeful ends, not merely a welter of changing circumstances. However much the progress of society may be challenged by the presence of giant evils still persisting in our world, it is an indisputable fact that over the ages there has been progress from the inorganic to the organic, from the animate to the sensient, from the sensient to the conscious, and from the conscious to the personal and human. There seems abundant evidence to affirm also that social progress is real, though the course has never been a steady upward climb, and luminous personalities have emerged along the way whose followers fell far below them.

If progress in any sense is a fact, then this is consistent with a guiding providence throughout the total scheme of things. For a belief in providence it is not necessary to maintain that everything is as God or man would have it; what is essential is to believe that creation at its foundations is good and that no evil is final or unmasterable by the grace and power of God.

The third thing to say is that empirically there is no reason to deny and every reason to affirm the biblical judgment as to the nature of man. Weak, sinful, and prone to error every man is, and one has only to look around, or better, to look *within* to find this to be true. Yet man is also a creature of infinite worth and dignity, with both actual achievements and potential capacities that mark him as supreme over all physical nature and all living things. Whence came man's mind and spirit that make him in a true sense a person save from the creative hand of a personal God? There is no satisfactory explanation in terms of undirected matter or a sub-human, impersonal force. Either the answer lies in the personal creativity of the God who made man in His own spiritual image, or no answer can be found.

This does not commit us to saying that we know exactly at what point in the evolutionary scale man emerged or by what processes in the mystery of God's creation man became distinct from the subhuman world as a living spirit. Sequences can properly enough be traced in the greater complexity of the nervous system, the development of the power of speech, the greater

77

facility of the hand, the power to walk erect. In man there are many biological similarities to and some important differences from the subhuman animal. Yet all these biological factors fall short of answering the basic question, "How did man come to be?" That man *is*, with the capacity for reflective thought, for moral judgments, for love and fellowship, for self-giving devotion to great ideals, for worship of the unseen is hardly to be questioned. There is no explanation in the type of thought which attempts to account for the distinctively personal in man by reducing him to a biological organism with an unusually complex nervous system.

Put together in our thinking these three basic constituents of the world which God has put together in reality, and where do we come out? A world of orderly processes, of purposeful advance, and of human personality may indeed be "the best of all possible worlds"—not the best *imaginable*, as these words in derision are often interpreted to mean—but the best possible in terms of the total structure. The world we have was graphically and rightly called by Keats "a vale of soul-making," and within it, in spite of personal frustrations and social retrogressions, an extraordinarily high level of spiritual, artistic, and cultural achievement has proved to be possible.

A world in which there was no opening up of fresh tasks, new possibilities of achievement on the basis of what has already been done, no permanency of acquisition, no heritage of the past of any sort, a world where every castle was of sand, to be washed away within a few hours by the tide, would be no fit place for personality to grow in.[10]

The experience of mankind gives evidence that highly worthful events have taken place and are continually occurring within the kind of world we have. It is not adapted to a painless or carefree existence; it *is* a fit place for personality to grow in.

Thus we are led, not by the Bible only but by observation of the

[10] Herbert H. Farmer, *op. cit.*, p. 299.

world as we find it, to the conclusion that a personal God is the Creator of the heavens and the earth; that this same God by a purposeful plan guides the course of created things and the destinies of men; that He has made us, though finite human beings, in kinship with Himself; that He has provided us a proper sphere for growth in the things of greatest worth. Yet sin and suffering remain, too much of both for any easy acquiescence in things as they are. The Christian faith affirms not only that God has created the world but that He "has visited and redeemed His people." To the study of redemption we turn in the next chapter.

Chapter Four

THE GOD WHO REDEEMS

IN THE PRECEDING CHAPTER WE SURVEYED BOTH THE BIBLICAL and the empirical grounds on which it is possible to affirm the goodness of creation by the God of Christian faith. No attempt was made to defend the view that in every aspect of human existence things are as they should be. Such an overoptimistic view is not warranted by the facts or called for by Christian faith. But neither is it realistic to maintain either a naturalistic view of the universe or a pessimistic view of human life. Such views are themselves "faiths" in the sense of chosen options based on selected elements of existence rather than the whole, though they fall short of being sustaining or lifting faiths in the presence of what their exponents regard as the cold indifference of the universe. At the best they look toward humanism, at the worst toward nihilism, and in between they present a secular view of life that fluctuates between superficial enjoyment and despair.

Christianity also, though affirming the goodness of creation by a good God, must reckon with the darker aspects of human existence. Theologians like philosophers must have something intelligible and constructive to say about the problem of evil or acknowledge defeat at a strategic sector of their thinking. Still more important is it for Christians, whether theologians or other people, to find power in God to master evil as it assails them in their living. If their Christian faith fails them at this point, it is likely to be suspected all around and dismissed by the skeptical as simply an inherited but relatively useless form of cultural conditioning.

We noted repeatedly in the previous chapter that according to the biblical faith, the God who creates is also the God who redeems, that the Creative Word is also the Redemptive Word. But from what evil do we need redemption? How does God redeem us? To these vital questions we now turn.

1. *From what do we need redemption?*

The word redemption means salvation. Every time the Lord's Prayer is spoken we pray, "Deliver us from evil." Redemption or salvation means deliverance from evil by the saving help of God. With the prefix "re" it suggests being brought back, and literally being "bought back," by God from a state of evil to His true design for us. Even the popular use of the term, as in the redemption of bonds or of a debt, indicates some recovery of value. This has a thread of connection with the Christian meaning, though the latter has a wealth of meaning not to be found in any monetary transaction. Christian redemption centers in a dual fact—first, *that evil exists,* and second, *that God is not content to leave us in it.*

Evil is many-sided, and were one to attempt to draw up a list of the various evils that infest mankind, the list would stretch on almost without end. Yet the major types of evil can be reduced to two or three. The kind of evil about which the Bible is most concerned is sin, with suffering as a tangent and subordinate though permeating fact of human existence. A third type of evil is not mentioned by name in the Bible, though being "dead through trespasses and sins" and coming to new life through Christ suggests it.[1] Indeed, there is no inclusive satisfactory term for it in English, but it is recognizable in the frustration of values, anxiety, inner unrest, loss of motivation and of "life" that dampens and defeats personality. The German word *angst* describes it more aptly than any single English word. This is often subsumed under either sin or suffering; yet it has qualities of its own which modern psychology and psychiatry have made evident. We shall now look at each of these types of evil in sequence and note something of their relations.

[1] Eph. 2:1; Col. 2:13.

a) *Sin.* There is perhaps no word in our language which is used more ambiguously, in spite of its apparent simplicity. To the ordinary secularist and to not a few Christians, to sin means to do what society condemns and in particular to indulge in the grosser sins of the flesh. In spite of a growing laxness of standards, to commit adultery, get drunk, steal money, or kill another human being calls forth condemnation in others and can arouse a guilty conscience and sense of sin in the person who does these things. That it often does not, through the ever-ready power of the human ego to rationalize and find excuses for its own behavior, does not alter the fact that many persons think of sin simply in these terms.

Sin to the understanding Christian means rebellion against God and disobedience to His holy will. Sin ought never to be defined moralistically, simply as deviation from accepted human standards. In contrast with the implicit moralism of much of American liberalism a generation ago, this view of sin as rebellion against God is now generally recognized by leaders of Christian thought. Yet it must persistently be made clear that the rejection of moralism means no repudiation of Christian morality. There is no true possibility of defining sin in relation to God by disregard of relations with one's fellow men, for God is intimately concerned with these same fellow men and obedience to Him requires of us Christian *agape* (self-giving love) toward them.

It would be a caricature of neo-orthodox thought, or of Pauline thought from which much of this is drawn, to say that in this point of view moral distinctions are irrelevant to sin. Yet there is a trend in this direction. I recall vividly the sense of shock with which I heard a German theologian some twenty years ago declare, "Sin has nothing whatever to do with morality!" I have read and heard many statements since that time which suggest this, though they do not usually say it quite so baldly. Even Emil Brunner, whose concern with Christian ethics is unquestioned, has written, "The contrast between virtue and vice has no relation to the fact of being either a pagan or a Christian. To be a pagan or a Christian is not related to the contrast between vice and virtue, but to that between sin and faith." [2] Carried to its logical conclusion, this would mean that the life of virtue is irrelevant to the life of faith. This I believe to be contrary to the teaching of Jesus and to the most valid insights of Christian faith.

Sin, then, is a relationship to God focused in self-centeredness, which shows itself in unloving attitudes and acts toward our fellow men. The neo-orthodox emphasis on sin as *pride*—a self-righteous arrogance where a humble abasement before God is called for, and the liberal emphasis on sin as *selfishness* meet at the point of man's self-centeredness. It is when we seek our own wills instead of God's will and regulate our lives by such self-seeking that sin corrupts our nature. This we all do. Thus, all men are sinners. Paul's insight, verified constantly throughout the Bible and empirically evident, is a true one, "none is righteous, no, not one." (Rom. 3:9).

Sin is rebellion against God, disobedience to the will of God. Yet some persistent questions remain. Is every act corrupted by sin? Are we the recipients of an inherited corruption, that is, of "original" sin? How did sin get into the world if not by the Fall of Adam?

These are large questions which must have at least a brief answer if the Christian doctrine of redemption is to be meaningful.

We need to distinguish, yet bring into relation, *sin* and *sins*. Sin is a state of self-centeredness; sins are particular acts, whether of thought or outward behavior, in which this self-centeredness is expressed in disobedience to God. That all men are in some degree self-centered, both before and after Christian conversion, is a patent fact. This does not justify a doctrine of total depravity, for not every impulse is self-centered, and in the Christian saint whose life is God-centered and love-centered there are amazing demonstrations of the power of God in Christ to conquer self-

[2] *The Christian Doctrine of Creation and Redemption, Dogmatics, II.,* (Philadelphia: Westminster Press, 1952), 110.

centeredness. Yet it remains true that no man is ever completely free from the power and presence of sin. As truly as "all men are mortal," so it can be affirmed that "all men are sinners."

Yet it is fallacious to assume from this that *every act* is sinful. There are pure thoughts; there are self-giving and even sacrificial deeds in which love is expressed and the will of God is done. One sees them in others; one ought to be hesitant about claiming them for himself. It is significant that no real saint ever thinks he is one. Yet there are Christian saints, and there are Christian acts about which, in humble gratitude to God, one does not need to be tortured by a guilty conscience.

The primary focus of Christian redemption lies in gaining moral and spiritual victory by the mercy and grace of God. To deny the reality of changed motives and courses of action is to invalidate redemption and reduce it to a mere emotional glow, or to some mysterious metaphysical change which bears no evident relation to the life of Christian virtue. We must insist that if redemption is real, so is the actual conquest of sin and the increase of goodness in human life.

Yet if all men are sinners, prone to self-centeredness, how did we get that way? Traditional Christian thought has affirmed an original state of innocence, corrupted by the Fall of Adam, and transferred by biological inheritance to every subsequent human being. In Roman Catholic thought this has produced the doctrine not only of the virgin birth of Jesus but the immaculate conception of Mary to guard our Lord from stain of sin, with much else in the sacramental system of salvation. In Protestant thought, until the rise of liberalism, a doctrine of original sin was imbedded with equal firmness, though the deductions drawn from it were different. What shall we do with it?

From the standpoint of biblical interpretation the first thing to note is that Adam means man in general, generic man rather than a single individual. The story of the Fall in the third chapter of Genesis, like the stories of creation in the first two, is a mythological rather than historical account of how sin entered the world. It is mythology with a meaning, and the story of man's presumption in seeking to be "like God" reflects vividly our human arrogance and self-righteousness.[3] However, few biblical scholars now take this story literally or believe that its fullest meaning can be found by doing so.

A less generally recognized fact is that the Bible itself makes very little reference to this story of the Fall. It does not appear again in the Old Testament. In the New Testament it is mentioned briefly in I Cor. 15:21, 22 and given detailed analysis by Paul in Rom. 5:12-21. It is on the basis of the latter, aided by a reference in Ps. 51:5 to being conceived in sin and brought forth in iniquity, that the doctrine of original sin has mainly rested. If Paul had not written what he did in Romans 5, it is safe to assume that Christian theology might have taken a very different course. But he did write it, and the doctrine developed.

The doctrine of original sin is best understood not biologically but as a description of our ongoing, natural, and never wholly conquered self-centeredness. A baby is not born a sinner, for there is no sin until there is some measure of freedom and moral responsibility. Yet every child is born with tendencies that, if not redirected, become sinful as the child grows to maturity. No child needs to be taught to grab another child's toys or assert its own little ego in clamant demands, showing off, or staging a tantrum; these tendencies have to be "educated out" of the child through wise parental care. If not, these infantilisms persist to become adult self-centeredness and sin. Baptism, whether in infancy or adult life, will not remove sin. Its purpose is to symbolize before God and the Christian community the intention of Christian nurture and of personal Christian commitment.

Sin, therefore, is "original" in the sense of a persistent human tendency, and the Fall of man happened not once but is a perpetual falling away from the life of loving obedience which God requires of us. To hold this view is frankly to abrogate the idea of any original state of innocence, once enjoyed but soon lost by man's first parents. Sin, as Reinhold Niebuhr has effectively

[3] Gen. 3:4, 5.

maintained, lies at the juncture of nature and spirit. To sin requires more than a biological organism. At whatever point in human development man became a free spirit, capable of rebellion against God, able to make morally responsible decisions, at that point sin entered the world. It has remained ever since, not biologically transmitted in the traditional sense of an inherited corruption, yet inborn in the sense that every person has self-centered and hence sinful tendencies.

Does this view make God the author of sin? The older view attempted to absolve God from responsibility by placing the blame on Adam, but it never actually succeeded since God remained the transmitter of the curse to each newborn child. Theories of creationism and traducianism[4] have been devised to take the responsibility from God and place it on the parents through the act of propagation. There is a lapse in logic in the attempt to amalgamate this view with the belief that each new child is the gift of God, and it has had the historic effect in Christian thought of relating sin particularly to the sexual act. The orthodox view, furthermore, appears to the modern mind as singularly immoral in placing on each innocent, newborn baby the curse of an ancient ancestor. But can an alternative view escape these dilemmas?

Any view of God as the Creator makes Him responsible for the *possibility* of sin. There is no way in which consistently to say that God is our Maker without also saying that He has made us with the capacity to sin. Yet if God has made us with a good purpose, the capacity to sin becomes not a curse but a blessing, for it is the mark of our freedom and our true dignity as persons. Inanimate objects do not sin. Subhuman animals do not sin. Only man sins, for sin lies at the juncture of nature and spirit, and only man is spirit, made in the image of God.

Sin exists only where there is freedom to feel, think, and act

[4] Creationism is the doctrine that God immediately creates each new human soul, while the child's body comes from the parents. Traducianism holds that both body and soul are passed on to the offspring, with the creation of man having occurred only once, on the sixth day of creation.

responsibly and hence to disobey God by overt defiance or by failure at the point where love ought to be. This is why no little child is a sinner, though self-centered tendencies are inborn. These same tendencies may also be seen as part of the wise and good providence of the Creator, that a child may reach out to his world and grow in the power of responsible choice. Without them a child might be as amenable to conditioning as a dog or a cat; he could not be a human being developing a personality through the interplay of biological, social, and inner spiritual forces.

It follows, therefore, that God is not the author of sin. With a fervor equal to Paul's we do well to exclaim, "Are we to continue in sin that grace may abound? By no means!" (Rom. 6:1-2.) Sin is real, and sin is the sinner's own responsibility. Any other view makes repentance meaningless. God in His infinite goodness has made us able to sin, able to repent, able to accept His freely offered forgiveness and grace. Lives can be changed, and lives are changed, from sin to service and moral victory. This great fact lies at the center of what redemption means.

b) *Suffering.* Though sin is the deeper aspect of the problem of evil, theoretically it presents fewer problems. Sin can be understood as man's misuse of the moral freedom given by God for a high purpose. Suffering, both of mind and body, remains a persistent fact which, in its total enormity, is less easily accounted for.

That human life should have some suffering in it for growth of personality and discipline of character is evident. It is not good for any child or adult to "have things too easy." Modern educational theories based on interest, enjoyment, and self-expression have much to commend them. But unless the self-discipline which is expected to accompany them is based on some acceptance of the stern necessities and unpleasant facts of life, unrestrained freedom tightens the bonds of self-centeredness to a worse imprisonment than the older forms of discipline produced. Much of the nervousness and tension of modern life can be traced to the "spoiled child" attitude of adults who have never learned to take suffering and grow thereby.

Suffering has also a function as a warning of situations that require correction. This is evident in physical pain that shows there is something wrong with one's body that had better be looked after. In a deeper and more pervasive sense, when things "get out of joint" in an individual's personality or in a community or in a great social group, corrective action is indicated.

Suffering can be redemptive. It can transform, enrich, and deepen the personality of the sufferer, as many have attested who have come through it to stronger living and a higher sense of the reality and the presence of God. Many of the greatest testimonies of Christian experience, both in literature and in life, are found in the words of those who have discovered in the midst of pain life's deeper meanings and God's grace sufficient to transcend suffering and transform its power. Furthermore, suffering voluntarily incurred in love for the service of others and in sharing of their pain is the way of the cross. Jesus chose this way and called his followers to walk in it. Such suffering love lies at the heart of Christian faith. Without it vast ranges of human experience would be infinitely poorer.

Yet there is too much pain in the world. Not only do some individuals seem marked for tragedy as if by a persistent fate, but there are mammoth breeders of suffering that any sane man, to say nothing of any Christian, would like to see eliminated. Complacency before them is the mark of moral dullness. Hunger and homelessness, poverty, injustice, disease, traffic accidents, broken homes, alcoholism, race prejudice, and war are among them. These can be traced, either directly or indirectly, to human sin, ignorance, moral dullness, and complacency. But there are also disastrous floods, earthquakes, tornadoes, and other physical phenomena that cause much loss of life and property without comparable benefit and which, by a curious twist of legal language, invading the province of theology, are called "acts of God." Can we say in reality that any of these are acts of God, and if so, how can we believe that a good God is the Creator and Controller of our world? In short how can we confront these facts and still believe in providence?

We shall not pretend to have found the complete answer. To quote Paul's language, "we see in a mirror dimly." Yet some things can be seen and ought to be seen and said.

Most of the suffering of the world can be traced to three major blessings granted us by a good God, which we would not surrender if we could, for without them human life, if it existed at all, would be unendurable. These are the gift to men of responsible choice through moral freedom, the orderliness of the physical world, and our interrelatedness in both spheres.

It is by our power of responsible choice that we are free to sin, either actively or by complacent acquiescence in preventable evil, thereby bringing suffering on ourselves and others. This is not to say that *all* the surplus suffering of the world could be prevented by human love, intelligence, and resolute action, but an enormous amount of it could be. To the degree that with our resources of talent, possessions, and opportunity we could make the world a less painful place to live in, and we fail to do so, we sin. The suffering then is man's fault, not God's.

The physical disasters are harder to understand. In an ultimate sense we must call them, as the insurance policies do for prudential reasons, acts of God. If they are not, something else besides God controls our world. Yet this is not to say that God acting in them is acting helplessly, blindly, or in indifference to human good. As was suggested in the previous chapter, a physical world of order and uniformity, within which, to a high degree, prediction is possible and about which scientific knowledge can be acquired, is an infinitely better world than a chaotic one would be. We cannot suppose that when the floods and the tornadoes come, God deliberately sends them to smite their victims with the wrath of His displeasure. Rather, they come through the operation of physical forces which, in their total structure, are beneficent. God must suffer in the suffering they cause more deeply then does any human heart, but to interrupt or set aside the orderly processes of His world would abrogate the chosen structure of His creation. To maintain this world of natural order, which the all-wise Creator has established for our good, God *permits* suffering even when we cannot say that in particular instances He *wills* it to occur.

At this point an important distinction, often overlooked, needs to be drawn. This is between the *power* and the *purpose* of God. The earthquakes and the hurricanes occur by the power of God. This we must say unless we are to suppose that they are caused by an indifferent nature outside of God's creativity and control or by some malevolent being more powerful than God. The first of these alternatives is at variance with the Christian doctrine of God as the Creator and Ruler of His world; the second, though it has some biblical basis and has been widely held by Christians, leaves unanswered the question as to how such a malevolent being, rivalling and even overruling the power of God, came into existence in God's world.[5]

If "this is my Father's world," as Christians not only sing but deeply believe, all that happens in nature happens by God's power. But this does *not* mean that everything happens by the specific will and purpose of God. This distinction is crucial. That it is the wise and good purpose of God to create and maintain an orderly world of nature we must believe; this does not obligate us to believe that every event that occurs within it is according to His purpose and therefore to be accounted good.

Yet this is not the whole story. Creation continues. Unless God finished His work on the sixth day of primordial time, there

[5] To many minds belief that all evil is the work of Satan answers the question more simply than any other solution. There are unquestionably references to Satan in the Bible, though significantly not until after the Exile, when this dualistic note was probably introduced into Hebrew thought from Zoroastrianism. Yet even if the existence of a rival malevolent power be admitted, this does not answer the metaphysical question of his origin. The traditional idea of the devil as a fallen angel has only a slight biblical basis in passages open to other interpretations, and granting their historicity, there is still the enormous problem of how the one, all-wise, all-powerful Creator could have thus let the devil "get out of hand" to constitute so formidable a rival to His own power. Though ground must be left for differing opinions as to the existence of a personal devil, it should be clear that to believe in his existence by no means solves the problem of evil.

is no barrier to the belief that God is still shaping the course of an unfinished world, within which He uses the services of men. While there is no reason to expect that human effort will ever alter the basic structure of the universe, every effort at flood control and architectural adjustment to the expectancy of earthquakes and storms gives evidence that natural disasters are not an inevitable fate. Even atomic energy is God's energy, to be used for human good.

God is not the helpless victim of evil forces beyond His control, nor is He an arbitrary and despotic celestial dictator. He is the Maker of heaven and earth, within which He has delegated to men enormous powers to work with Him or to thwart His ongoing creativity. A large part of God's redemptive work is the power and the motivation He imparts to men to labor for the elimination of preventable suffering.

Yet so long as men are bound to one another and bound to nature as the material framework of human living, some suffering will continue. This interrelatedness is again a blessing no one would willingly surrender if he could. Without the possibility of harming one another there could be no helpfulness; no family love, no fellowship, no immediate or world-wide neighborliness could exist without it. Similarly, without the risk of accident and injury, there could be no utilization of the physical and chemical processes on which so much of life depend. We cannot have it both ways, and if we are to rejoice in the gifts of God, we must take the hazards with them.

To choose one simple illustration from among many, take the family automobile. There can be no family joys without the possibility of family sorrows; there can be no use of so useful an instrument without some risk. In this use within this fellowship accidents that are serious and tragic sometimes occur. When an irresistible force meets an immovable object, something smashes, and it may be the body of the person we love best. Under such circumstances there is no necessity to call this tragedy the will of God. Because the kind of world that He has made is the sphere of our highest joys and usefulness, God permits much that He does not will. Our function is to do our utmost by His help to reduce the hazard and pain of existence, and when it comes, to find our strength in His companionship and never-failing love.

There is a persistent tendency to feel that God's providence is meaningless unless a specific divine purpose for good can be seen—or at least can be believed to be present—in every specific event that brings suffering with it. Why did the automobile accident happen *to me?* Why did *my child* contract polio? Why did the hurricane hit *my house?* These questions recur incessantly. The most common answer from a Christian standpoint is, "It was the will of God. We must accept it, though we do not understand."

That there is mystery beyond our understanding, and that facts must be accepted as they are, is undisputable. But that such events must be viewed as coming from the particular will and purpose of God is contrary to all that this book attempts to say. The assumption that God wills everything to happen just as it does is predestinarian; its logical outcome is that "whatever is, is right." When such suffering is the result of preventable circumstances, it is little less than blasphemy to attribute it to the will of God.

We may well believe that God seeks always, with the cooperation of His human children, to eliminate unnecessary and unredemptive suffering. Yet this is only one side of God's action. His major gift is not freedom from pain but the power and peace by which any suffering can be endured and turned to spiritual triumph. Some suffering can be understood, some cannot. Some can be eliminated, some cannot. There is much that must be endured, but it is the witness of twenty centuries of Christian faith that neither stoical endurance nor defeat is the Christian answer. It was the same Christian who could say, "We know that the whole creation has been groaning in travail together until now," who could also say, "We know that in everything God works for good with those who love him." (Rom. 8:22, 28.) It was also this same Christian who had a thorn in the flesh, which he calls "a messenger of Satan" to harass him, who prayed earnestly to have it removed but instead heard the voice of God saying to him, "My grace is sufficient for you, for my power is made perfect in weakness." (II Cor. 12:7-9.) Though it would be uncharitable to be glad that Paul had to be troubled with this persistent, nagging pain, this testimony to God's redemptive word and work in the presence of it has helped countless millions of other Christians.

c) *Frustration.* I suggested earlier that sin and suffering are not the only kinds of evil from which we need redemption. There is a third borderline form of evil which is sinful if it is voluntarily harbored, but it may not be subject to the will; it may induce acute mental pain even to the point of insanity but may take the form simply of dullness and loss of nerve. For lack of a single covering term I shall call it frustration, for it always involves failure to achieve cherished values, but it goes by a variety of terms which, without being synonyms, each suggests some angle of it. From a psychological point of view it is apt to be termed neurosis, depression, or some form of personality maladjustment, while theologians may refer to it as alienation, estrangement, or "the dark night of the soul." It takes many forms not to be superficially identified with each other, but these have a common center in being the opposite of "peace of mind." It is a very persistent malady in our time, and much of the current "cult of reassurance" is directed toward it.

This is too complex a phenomenon for discussion here in more than the barest outline. However, it is important to point out a number of relevant facts. The first of these is that such a condition cannot be met simply by regarding it as sin, requiring repentance and forgiveness, or as sickness, requiring physical and mental treatment. Elements of both may indeed be present, but the admixture of each requires great skill in diagnosis and counseling. The second is that any real help that can be given, whether or not it is under religious auspices, whether or not it is a full expression of the Christian gospel, ought to be gladly welcomed.[6] The third and most important fact is that there is no full or final answer to this state of inner unrest apart from the depths of the divine mercy and the life-transforming power of Christian faith. Jesus, as he moved among men driving out the demons of unrest, healing bodies and souls, forgiving sins and imparting new life, gave no easy remedy or soft way out of life's perplexities and deadness. Any proffered help fails to be really helpful unless it both inspires hope and makes costing demands.

In an earlier book, *The Dark Night of the Soul*,[7] I have said what I believe it most essential to say and what can be said from a layman's standpoint on this baffling form of evil. Severe instances of it require psychiatric help, but in many cases a religious counselor can help the person to the spiritual victory he needs. In dealing with this situation, whether in one's self or another, both coddling and over-condemnation must be avoided. The physical and social causes of the trouble must be looked for and if possible corrected. Attention needs to be projected outward and expressed in appropriate service. Self-understanding is essential, and the understanding love of family and friends can do much to alleviate the spiritual darkness. But above all one must know that God is with him in the dark, even when the clouds cut off any conscious awareness of His presence. If one will trust in God and wait in hope, he can come out on the far side of his morass to brighter days and firmer foundations than before.

2. How does God redeem us?

Up to this point in the chapter we have been seeking an answer to the question, "From what do we need redemption?" This query has made it necessary to canvass some basic issues relevant to the problem of evil. Already some suggestions have been made as to how God redeems us, or more accurately, through what

---

[6] For example such books as Rabbi Joshua Loth Liebman's *Peace of Mind* and Norman Vincent Peale's *The Power of Positive Thinking* and *A Guide to Confident Living* ought to be appreciated for their helpfulness to a great number of persons instead of being disparaged for what they lack.

[7] Nashville: Abingdon Press, 1945.

channels the Christian may in faith look for God's redemptive action. Though no human mind can probe the mystery of God's grace from God's end—and it would be blasphemy to attempt it—it is nevertheless possible to see God at work within the world's evil, turning it to good. We must now look more closely at these many "means of grace."

a) *Natural grace.* To some "natural grace" is a contradictory use of terms, or at least a term to be used only nontheologically as descriptive of the natural gracefulness of children or other unspoiled living creatures. The latter, though real enough, is not what we are here concerned with. In a theological sense those who reject natural theology reject also natural grace and find the redemptive activity of God only in Jesus Christ. However, those who find in the created world, as well as in the incarnate Son, a manifestation of God's agape-love are not so likely to balk at the idea of natural grace. This synthesis is the position maintained throughout this book.

Two cautions are in order. The first is the need to be clear that nature is not something independent of God, self-caused and self-existent. It is the all-wise and all-good Creator, not some impersonal and indifferent force, that is the source of natural grace. The entire preceding chapter was an attempt to give reasons for this faith. The second caution is the need to observe that nature, as the term is used in this connection, means both physical and human nature, though not with a naturalistic interpretation of either. When we speak of natural grace, we mean the grace that comes to men through the entire created world of men and things in interplay with each other.

With this understanding the Christian need not hesitate to affirm the existence of natural grace, for it is but to restate the goodness of creation from the hand of God. It is to fix attention on the creative and curative factors that God has strewn so bountifully throughout His world. One finds it in friendship and human love, and particularly in the sustaining and healing power of family affection. One finds it in the power of the injured body to regain health, to reknit severed bones and tissues,

95

and to readjust to radical internal and outward changes. One finds it even more mysteriously, but not less certainly, in the healing touch of time, whereby the grief of bereavement or the shattering of old securities can be transcended and a new life fashioned. One finds it in the joy of parenthood with the coming of young life into the world; one finds it, though mixed with pain, in the boon of death, whereby an all-wise God removes the old that young life may go forward. Death that comes prematurely or violently we do well to attribute to causes other than God's will, and we must seek to prevent it; death in senility when a life has run its course and its work is done may well be ascribed to the wise beneficence of our Creator.

When one sets out to enumerate the elements in human existence that reveal God's bounty and provide channels of natural grace, the list becomes almost endless. We are born into a world of beauty—a world that poets sing about and plain men rejoice in unless their vision is too clouded. There is the entire world of truth, beckoning us on to appropriate the wisdom of the past and to make new ventures into the unknown. There is adventure of body, mind, and spirit. There is sunshine and fresh air, the good earth, food to eat, and enough for all within the resources of the earth. There is work to do, which in God's providence ought not to be merely dull drudgery but creative achievement. There is leisure, relaxation, and play, and although these opportunities like work and material possessions are too often unjustly distributed among the world's millions, the possibilities are present awaiting human adjustment and appropriation.

One ought not to rhapsodize over the goodness of the world without taking account of these inequalities of distribution. Nothing is gained by a person who is healthy, comfortable, and secure telling another who is sick, hungry, poor, or overburdened that he ought to forget all this and think of the goodness of God's world! Much human effort is still needed before all can enjoy to the full the bounty of God's creation. Yet bountiful it is, and there is natural grace in great abundance in the world

God has provided as the dwelling place for His human children. Were there no other grounds of faith, these facts alone would justify a doctrine of divine providence.

b) *The grace of God in Jesus Christ.* It is not in natural grace that the heart and center of God's redemptive goodness can be found. Christians and non-Christians alike have access to the bounties freely given by God in physical and human nature. Yet there are dark clouds of sin, suffering, and frustration that overshadow this natural goodness and often hide it from our sight. No such superficial optimism as is expressed in the cliché, "Every cloud has a silver lining," or other injunctions to cheerfulness by holding the right thought, will really meet and illumine the darkness of existence. Only God in Christ does that.

This is not to say that Christianity alone is the channel of God's grace. Every high religion ministers in some form to the spiritual needs of men. If it did not, it would atrophy and disappear, or at best become simply a matter of conventional social practice. "Religion," wrote Alfred Whitehead, "is the vision of something which stands beyond, behind, and within the passing flux of immediate things." [8] This vision is not limited to Christianity and is found in the devout worship of those of many faiths. Regarding both the material and the spiritual gifts of God, we may well believe that God "did not leave Himself without witness" among any people (Acts 14:17). There is a telling answer to any narrow religious parochialism in Paul's words to the Greeks on Mars Hill:

And he made from one every nation of men to live on all the face of the earth, having determined alloted periods and the boundaries of their habitation, that they should seek God, in the hope that they might feel after him and find him. Yet he is not far from each one of us, for "In him we live and move and have our being"; as even some of your poets have said, "For we are indeed his offspring."

(*Acts 17:26-28.*)

[8] *Science and the Modern World* (New York: Macmillan Co., 1925), p. 267.

97

Yet it is untrue to say that man's vision of God or God's downreach to man in redemptive love is found equally in all faiths. There was no blurring of distinctions in Paul's theology, and there ought not to be in ours. In Jesus Christ alone is the full, complete, and adequate channel of God's redemptive grace.

How does Jesus Christ redeem us? Again we cannot say in any ultimate sense, for the mystery is too great for any finite human wisdom, but we can point to some ways in which we know Him as Redeemer. The fact of redemption as it is seen in lives changed by the love of Christ is unmistakable. Sinners become faith-filled, loving, and morally victorious over temptation; the weak become strong; the fearful brave; the suffering find spiritual triumph over pain and a firm forward look; the distraught find peace; the dull of heart find new life and zest for living. All in all, "if any one is in Christ, he is a new creation." (II Cor. 5:17.) From this indisputable, experienced fact, from almost twenty centuries of Christian history, and from the Bible we can draw such knowledge of redemption as we need.

Liberal Christian thought has, on the whole, tended to stress the life, ministry, and teachings of Jesus, while orthodoxy, both old and new, has found the focus of Christ's redemptive work in his death upon the cross. So far has this latter tendency been carried that to not a few Christians, "the blood" would appear to be virtually all that matters. However, it is not necessary to choose between the life and the death of Christ, for they belong together. Any stress upon one to the exclusion of the other is bound to lead to distortion and to weaken the great meaning that inheres in both.

When we look at the ministry and teaching of Jesus as it is set forth—probably not with complete accuracy but with portraiture that rings true—in the Gospels, several impressions are inescapable. Here is a man of remarkable religious insight and devotion to God, whose one and only purpose was to serve God in faith and love and bring others to that faith and love. Here is a man of boundless compassion, healing the bodies, minds, and souls of men through God-given powers beyond that of any ordinary person. Here is one who taught the love of God and neighbor with such pungency and aptness that his words were remembered long after his death, and are still quoted as a guide to conduct in our day. Here is one indifferent to popular acclaim and willing completely to thwart popular hopes of a political Messiah, who nevertheless apparently believed himself to be the long-expected Deliverer, chosen by God as His own beloved Son to bring redemption to men. Here is one who, after changing the lives of an unknown number of individuals and training a little band of followers to carry on his work, died in complete fidelity to his God-given mission, and on the third day rose again.

Had we no other witness to the redemptive work of Jesus Christ, this record would be enough to set him apart from all other individuals and give him the foremost place in history. his living and his teaching set before us a way which, if followed seriously, would transform the world. No man can hope fully to "imitate Christ," but to follow him in Christ-like fidelity, obedience, and service is the major need of every age and society.

Yet this is not all. It was the conviction of the early Church, which ought also to be ours, that "God shows his love for us in that while we were yet sinners Christ died for us" (Rom. 5:8). God was in Christ, and because the death of Christ upon the cross was that of no ordinary man or religious genius but the Son of God Himself, by His death He has "opened the kingdom of heaven to all believers."

The cross means first, the climax and culmination of a life of God-centered service in love, the meeting point of love with suffering that is not simply inevitable, but freely chosen. Jesus could have evaded the cross, but he would not then have been our Lord. He led the way in suffering love, and any man who would truly follow him must deny himself and take up his cross and follow him.

But the cross of Christ is more than our pattern and example; it is the event in which God gave Himself freely and unreservedly for the salvation of mankind. "He who did not spare his own

99

Son but gave him up for us all, will he not also give us all things with him?" (Rom. 8:32.) Though all efforts at logical description fail us, the Christian knows that in the cross and resurrection God has released a power that conquers sin and death. Rightly we observe Good Friday and Easter as the focal days that give meaning to all the rest of the Christian year.

The cross is our pattern of love-filled, faithful service; it is the supreme event whereby God gave, and still gives, power to meet any evil that may assail us. It is therefore both symbol and expression of what God is always doing for mankind. All that can be said about evil meets its final answer, not in any theoretical justification of the ways of God with man, but in the demonstration of His eternal love that shines from the cross.

Yet the cross is not God's last word and need not be ours. After Good Friday comes Easter, and joy and triumph and God's victory over sin and death. Let us not forget that the first Good Friday, when Jesus hung with thieves on Calvary and was crucified for the sins of the world, did not seem very good. It was very dark indeed to his disciples, who had forsaken him and fled at his arrest, and whose shattered hopes are expressed with great poignancy in the words, "But we had hoped that he was the one to redeem Israel" (Luke 24:21). Though Jesus had spoken great words about eternal life and had foretold his own resurrection, with their own earthly future now so uncertain all this was apparently forgotten. Despair had gripped them.

Then something happened! Early on the first Easter morning the women who loved him went to the tomb. There they learned that death had been conquered! Over my desk hangs a picture of Gutzon Borglum's "Mary Magdalene." The light of glad expectancy and renewed hope is in her eyes as she turns from the empty tomb to confront the Living Christ. In one word, "Rabboni!" are compressed her gratitude, her enduring devotion, her joy. For her triumph was shining through grief, and hope had been born.

And so it was with the other followers of Jesus when this great, glad news was known. Again and again he appeared to them until even the skeptical Thomas could no longer doubt. Gone were confusion, frustration, and despair! The little company "came alive" with news about which they could not be silent. It was a gospel of faith and hope and love through the gift of God in Jesus Christ. In Him God had conquered sin and death and had called them to be His witnesses. It was in this resurrection faith that the Christian Church was born.

We are today the inheritors of this resurrection faith which no persecution or pain could daunt. To us, as to those first Christians, has been committed a gospel of triumph over sin and death through Christ, the hope of the world.

c) *Eternal life.* And what of eternal life? There are many things about it we should like to know. But God, through His Son, has given us all the knowledge we need to have. What, then, may we know with full assurance? We shall intimate this here, then look further in a later chapter.

First, eternal life is not solely a matter of endless time; it is a quality of life. It is the kind of life to which Jesus calls us, and this may begin here and now, where we are. It is a life of surrender and loving obedience to the Son who has come to show us the Father. It is a joyous and invigorating, though a demanding, life. The word of Jesus to the woman at the well is still His word to us, ". . . Whoever drinks of the water that I shall give him will never thirst; the water that I shall give him will become in him a spring of water welling up to eternal life" (John 4:14).

But to say that eternal life begins here and now for the Christian is not all. It is a deeply grounded, confident note in our Christian faith that eternal life means life beyond the grave. As God has raised up Christ, so too He gives us eternal life beyond the gates of death and joy in His nearer Presence. Thus we can confront the inevitable fact of death for ourselves and our loved ones with courage and a great hope. The words recorded as spoken by Jesus to his disciples in the upper room are spoken also to us, "Let not your hearts be troubled; believe in God, believe also in me. In my Father's house are many rooms; if it were not so, would I have told you that I go to prepare a place for you? . . . Because I live, you will live also" (John 14:1-2, 19).

Our hope in Christ includes, but goes beyond, the hope of individual survival. Eternal life means also the hope of the coming of God's Kingdom on earth, as men accept His kingly rule, and a final victory beyond all boundaries of time and space. This earth must certainly be important to God, and what we do here in our relations with other men matters greatly. But it is not all-important. Men might mar our earthly society to the point where sin and strife would cause all life to be annihilated upon this planet, and still God would not be defeated.

This is our gospel of redemption, with a great hope for this life and the next. We can afford to be silent about some aspects of the mystery of evil and say with Job, "I lay my hand on my mouth" (Job 40:4) provided we have a gospel of salvation about which we cannot be silent. Such a gospel we have in the life, the death, the resurrection, and living presence of Jesus Christ our Lord.

So we affirm again that the God who creates is also the God who redeems. With the God and Father of our Lord Jesus Christ as our bulwark against evil and our sure foundation, no Christian need despair. Nothing in all creation will be able to separate us from the love of God in Jesus Christ our Lord.

Chapter Five

DIVINE SOVEREIGNTY AND HUMAN FREEDOM

IN THE TWO PRECEDING CHAPTERS WE HAVE SEEN REASONS TO believe that God is the Creator of a world that in its essential structure is good, though this is not to deny the presence of evil within it, and that the redemptive action of God seeks ever to deliver us from evil. This redemptive work, the gift to men of God whose nature is perfect love, is seen both in His beneficent endowment of natural grace and supremely in the life, ministry, death, and resurrection of His Son Jesus Christ. Hence, there is no ultimate or unconquerable evil, though there is much along our earthly path that God summons men to work with Him to eradicate. The final defeat of evil may well be believed to lie not within but beyond our earthly life and human history; yct the victory has already been won by the self-giving love of Jesus Christ our Lord.

In surveying these basic notes in Christian theology, it may have seemed to the reader that we were getting away from the central theme of providence as this was defined in the first two chapters. On the contrary nothing very fruitful can be said about providence except as this is placed in the wider setting of the nature of God and His relation to men.

We have not thus far made much reference to a term that looms large in most theological discussions of predestination and often of providence, namely, the sovereignty of God. Nor has reference been made explicitly to the phrase that occurs most often in ordinary speech in regard to God's rulership of human affairs, "God willing!" How are we to think of God's ruling and overruling the decisions and destinies of men?

That God is the sovereign Lord of human destinies and that man is in some sense a free spirit are foundation stones of Christian faith. These two affirmations do not comprise the whole of Christian theology, but they make all the rest of it an organic structure. Remove either of these foundations, and the structure either collapses or requires extraneous props for its support.

It is an elementary principle of architecture that the weight of a building must be distributed, if not evenly upon its foundation, at least in proper balance, with due regard to tensions and strains. The history of Christian thought could be written in terms of a never-ending attempt to keep a Hebrew-Christian concept of divine sovereignty in such relations with a Greek-Christian concept of human freedom as to render the structure able to bear the weight that faith and experience place upon it. Whenever there has been a marked weakening of either support, as in some aspects of current neo-Calvinism and in humanistic forms of liberalism, the result has been an aberration which, though called Christian by its exponents, has been a long way removed from authentic Christian thought.

1. The meaning of sovereignty and freedom

What is to be understood by the terms sovereignty and freedom? If the divine sovereignty means the complete, unqualified, even arbitrary omnipotence of God, then obviously He determines everything that happens in the human as well as in the inanimate or subhuman world, and there is no freedom. If human freedom is at no point subject to God's control, and God is powerless to affect man's life or destiny, then for all practical purposes atheism has triumphed. God as an abstract principle or as the object of aesthetic or intellectual contemplation might remain but not the living God of Christian faith.

Sovereignty and freedom, therefore, must be so understood that each term qualifies the other and makes possible a vital synthesis. Paradox we cannot hope fully to eliminate, for there is much in Christian faith that appears to be contradictory. In

104

such matters as the divine-human nature of Christ, the transcendence and the immanence of God, the dignity and the sinfulness of man, a resolution of opposites can be found only at the deeper levels of faith and experience. Yet paradox must not be made an excuse for sheer inconsistency and self-contradiction. If both sovereignty and freedom are to be affirmed, they must be affirmed in a way that makes possible their union.

By the sovereignty of God I mean the power of God so to initiate action and control events that man may rightly look to Him as the Lord of life and Ruler of human destiny. Such sovereignty is compatible with a measure of self-limitation on the part of God and therefore is not to be equated with complete or unqualified omnipotence.

An important distinction, often overlooked, must be drawn between a *self-limited* and a *finite* God. A self-limited God is one who, in His infinite wisdom and goodness, has chosen to create a world of natural order and human freedom. In such a world, which He maintains with consistency and with constancy of purpose, some events occur which are not in accordance with His will and which must be judged by both man and God to be evil circumstances requiring challenge and amelioration. The goodness of such a world does not depend on each particular event but on the fact that a haphazard world of human robots would be unfitted to fulfill God's high purpose for mankind. A finite God, on the other hand, is one believed to be limited by some force outside of God's power and purpose in creation—a rival deity or a malevolent being or a "Given" in God's own nature against which He has to struggle. This last alternative, advocated with much earnestness and acumen by my honored teacher, the late Edgar S. Brightman, deals with great seriousness with the problem of evil. But does it solve it? In my judgment this view implies a limitation in the nature of God which is not consistent with belief in "God the Father Almighty" as the source of all created things. It preserves the goodness by constricting the power of God in a manner less satisfactory than does the belief that God is self-limited.

105

The term divine sovereignty is not the happiest that could be used to designate God's control over the fortunes and destinies of men. It suggests too much the idea of political authority. Yet it is imbedded in theological language and indirectly has a biblical base. Jesus' central message was that of the Kingdom, and kingship implies sovereignty. Rather than reject the term, we need to put into it content which is true both to the insights of the Bible and to our own experience.

That God is the Ruler of His world can hardly be doubted without denying our right and obligation to call Him Lord. That is what lordship means. He is the supreme object of loyalty and devotion; He has ultimate authority over all that He has made. To refuse to acknowledge God's ultimate sovereignty is to dethrone Him and put in His place some idol such as the State, the demands of money-getting in the economic order, or some private but dearly prized desire. He is, as Oliver Wendell Holmes put it, "Lord of all being, throned afar," and the central note of the Christian faith is the call to exalt Him as Lord of all and serve Him in obedient love.

Yet the sovereign Lord of all is not a dictator or an arbitrary despot. In His infinite wisdom and goodness He has given to men the power of free and responsible decision, taking the risk that men would thwart His will by sin and, we may believe, well aware that this was bound to happen. The sovereignty of God, though it means ultimate control of human affairs as well as of the physical universe, does not mean coercion. We are free to reject His providence and mar our destiny.

Nevertheless, man is never wholly free. I have already suggested how far an individual's destiny and the choices he can make in pursuit of it are constricted by circumstances. Some of these limitations, but only some, are the result of an individual's own previous acts and decisions. Many are caused by natural and social forces which he did not make but to which he must submit or adjust himself as best he can. What is the relation of God's sovereignty to these forces?

106

2. God's sovereignty in creation

God is the author of, and therefore has authority over, His created universe. Physical nature must not be identified with God in any pantheistic fashion but neither must it be divorced from His sovereign control. Wrestle as we may with the problem of the suffering caused by famines, floods, and hurricanes, we cannot say that these things happen independently of God's sovereign power, though we can say that for a higher purpose He permits the order of nature to be maintained even when individuals suffer from it. It is not that God puts abstract orderliness before human happiness; it is that human happiness and well-being are, on the whole, best conserved by the kind of world that God has made and continues to maintain.

The question of miracles will be examined in a later chapter. But we must anticipate enough to emphasize that nature is not an inflexible system that imprisons both God and man. In human experience man at almost every moment uses the laws of nature to express purposes, as I at this moment am using physical processes in conjunction with my typewriter to express certain ideas, and the potential reader uses other visual and neural processes to apprehend these words. If man can thus express and pursue purposes without violating the laws of nature, may not God also? Yet there are limits beyond which apparently God does not go, and it is not to impugn His providential care to say that He works within a structure of natural order we must not expect Him to violate or set aside.

Creation continues, and man's responsibility appears in the fact that Jesus conceived his mission as one of creative work to do the Father's will and called upon his followers to engage with him in labors of creative love. The sublime fact of divine initiative that is stated in the word, "In the beginning God created—" is not set aside but given new richness of meaning by "My Father is working still, and I am working" (John 5:17).

Throughout the ongoing creative process both God and man are working, with man sometimes aiding, sometimes thwarting the purposes of God. The social and dynamic character of creation is seen most clearly in divine-human effort for a better society, within which such major evils as war, tyranny, race prejudice, poverty, hunger, and disease are challenged, and some changes for the better, though slowly and painfully wrought, are brought about. This is by no means the full meaning of the coming of God's Kingdom, but in God's eyes these may well be steps toward that redeemed society in which His reign will be acknowledged by all men.

Even in the inanimate world creation continues through the work of God and man. Every change brought about in nature is a change for or against the purposes of God. This fact ought to give a high sense of stewardship in the use of material resources, not solely for economic advantage based on self-interest but for the maximum increase in human good. "The earth is the Lord's and the fulness thereof" (Ps. 24:1), and when so regarded, all nature may be viewed with religious reverence as the meeting place of God and man for a mutual task.

Almost anything in our experience with nature could be used as illustrative of this truth—soil conservation, better modes of agriculture for making "the good earth" yield its fruit, a thousand forms of technology for the production of goods to satisfy human wants. But nothing else so graphically illustrates man's potential creativity under God or his potential thwarting of the divine will as does atomic power. That which human inventiveness and discovery have produced for destructiveness, with all its ghastly possibilities of destroying the human race, has also almost unlimited possibilities for human service when turned to peaceful ends. Atomic energy is God's energy to be held and used in stewardship to Him.

When viewed from this perspective, nature is good and so is man's free, though constricted, relation to it. I must repeat that this is by no means to say that everything in nature is good or that all events occur as God would have them. There are bacteria which cause disease—horrible and hideous disease often snuffing out human life too soon, and there are predatory tendencies in animals, subhuman as well as human, which have led some to see nature chiefly as "red in tooth and claw." Nothing is gained by denying these facts, and while these phenomena may in a measure be explained as part of the total evolutionary structure of animate life, an element of mystery remains. It is important not to deny them or to overaccent them or to pretend fully to explain them. What is essential is to see that in spite of their presence God is good, nature is on the whole beneficent, and God gives us plenty of creative work to do for the conquest of evil elements.

Thus, we shall not expect to find a particular divine purpose reflected in every particular event. Rather, we shall do better to see the providence of God bringing good out of what appears to be the most evil circumstances and calling us to submit our wills to His for the continuance of His creative enterprise.

3. God's sovereignty in judgment

There is a close relation between God's sovereignty in creation and God's sovereignty in judgment. As a foundation for understanding the latter we must carry a step further the question as to how God creates.

There are three principal analogies under which the work of creation may be conceived. These are the work (1) of a technician or inventor making a machine, (2) of an artist calling into being a work of beauty, and (3) of a parent procreating and rearing a child.

Christian thought has rejected the technician idea, since this presupposes that God would simply be carrying out the plans and directions devised by some other mind. But it is not so clear that it has rejected the idea of a divine inventor. In fact deism comes very close to it. Deism regards God as having planned and brought into existence a world which, once made, runs mechanically except for occasional interventions. Though this is no longer often explicitly defended by philosophers or theologians, the implications of deism crop up repeatedly in discussions of miracles, special providences, and answers to prayer in a world assumed to have been made by God to run by itself according to the requirements of natural law.

To the degree that deism posits an "absentee God," there is no place in it for divine judgment except as God intervenes to smite sinners with the wrath of His displeasure. This has often been held to along with the idea of divine interventions imparting special blessings. This view receives support from many passages in the Bible which seem to indicate special occasions of divine displeasure as well as blessing, and it is assumed in interpreting these that "special" means "ab extra" (from without). Yet the primary note in the Bible is that in spite of varied forms of disclosure, culminating in His supreme revelation in Jesus Christ, the eternal God is *always present* and *always acting* within human events and human history.

Another legacy from deism, though based on recoil from such specific divine intervention, is the idea of automatic judgment. That there is a moral order in the universe, as certainly present as the physical order though less precisely predictable, is an important and valid note. But this is quite different from saying, as is sometimes stated and often implied, that judgment comes automatically upon the wrongdoer. If God is personal, He is always personally present in both judgment and redemption.

We conclude, therefore, that deism is no sufficient basis for linking the relations of divine sovereignty to human freedom. Though Christians sometimes hold to it and claim for it biblical sanction, it is at bottom unbiblical and unchristian.

But what of the idea of the divine artist? This has on the face of it less Christian ground to stand on than the idea of the divine inventor, though actually it has more. The idea of God as divine artist is not explicitly stated in the Bible, but it is there by implication in much of the great nature poetry. When we are told that the Spirit of God moved upon the face of the waters and God said, "Let there be light," we are dealing not only with a poetic statement of what happened but with a poetic conception of the nature of creativity. One gathers the same impression from the voice that speaks to Job out of the whirlwind and from many of the most majestic psalms.

A poet, as one who is familiar with the Greek etymology of the word will recall, means a "maker." A poet, if he is to be more than a mere rhymster, must create something, and what he creates must have a structure in which the parts are related to the whole. The created work must not only possess beauty but transmit meaning—a meaning not too obviously or didactically stated, but nevertheless present. What the poet creates must come out of his own personality, yet be projected to meet the response of other appreciative persons. The poem, if it is to live, must possess universality of meaning, leaving the reader or the listener with a sense of having been lifted out of himself and upward toward what is ultimately real.

These things, it may now be observed, are what God does in the making of His world. God creates a world of interrelated structure, of beauty of form, of oft-hidden but majestic meaning, of self-revelation to kindred minds, of eternal significance which lifts the religious spirit upward and outward to new heights of goodness, truth, and beauty. If God does this, we are entitled to speak of Him not only in terms of fatherly care but of artistic creativity.

This analogy, helpful though I believe it to be in understanding the general structure of creation, is incomplete at an important point. How does a great work of poetry judge us? By revealing our own lack of discernment if we are too dull to appreciate it, by stabbing us perhaps with a sense of inadequacy if we do. Great art, and in particular great drama, not only lifts but purges and condemns. Thus far the analogy of God as divine artist holds. Yet it does not hold all the way, for it is at the point of the personal, yearning, even suffering concern of Him who judges that the analogy is incomplete. We must move from it to something deeper for an understanding of the relation of God's sovereignty to our freedom.

It is the analogy of divine fatherhood that is most central to Christian thought, and it is this which most helpfully throws light

111

on the relations of divine sovereignty in judgment as well as in creation.

Jesus by his symbol of fatherhood set aside much that is monarchial in the Old Testament idea of God. Even had he not used the term Father for God, it would still be the metaphor best suited to express the relations of divine control to human freedom.

A child is begotten by his parents with no freedom on his part to say yes or no to the initial act of procreation. It is the parents' responsibility, not the child's, to see that the child is born with as healthy a body as possible and is reared under conditions of physical, mental, and social well-being. Persons who are good and wise enough to deserve to be parents must nourish, protect, govern, instruct, inspire, counsel, reward, and upon occasion punish the child. But all to one end, that the child may develop a free personality able to use this freedom for the best possible life. It is a paradoxical but ever-repeated fact that while some limitation of freedom is necessary for growth, the more coercion and consequent loss of initiative in the child, the less growth. The surest way to defeat the ends for which the human family exists is to try to be a dictator.

Though God's freedom, and therefore, God's responsibility, are infinitely greater than those of any human parent, the analogy can be drawn with a high degree of relevance. God's fatherhood requires that he take the initiative in creation and providence, that He lead his children along with infinite patience and at great cost to Himself and to them, that He delegate to them all the freedom they can use and some that they may misuse, that He never cease to care for them "like as a father pitieth his children." Within such a structure God can be both loving and severe. But God cannot be both loving and arbitrarily revengeful.

This is to say that God as Father is sovereign in the sense that he exercises supreme and loving control over the world. But never can he be a vindictive despot if He is "the God and Father of our Lord Jesus Christ." Herein lies the primary difference between judgment in the Christian sense and judgment in any sub-

112

Christian form. In Christian faith God's first purpose and God's last word is never judgment but mercy.

It is at this point that God's sovereign rule in a moral order, conceived not as an automatic system but as the expression of God's personal and redemptive concern, becomes relevant. It is a familiar, though often unrecognized, fact that to break the laws of God is to be broken upon them. Not all suffering is caused by sin; it has numerous other sources. Yet it is impossible for an individual, a racial or economic group, or a nation to sin without suffering the consequences. If not positive suffering or bodily death, then disintegration and decay result so that repeatedly the truth of Paul's word has been proved in experience, "The wages of sin is death." The only effective answer is found in the remainder of this quotation, "but the free gift of God is eternal life in Christ Jesus our Lord" (Rom. 6:23). Even when the penitent sinner receives the free gift of God's grace and the course of his life is changed thereby, the scars of sin in social and even in physical consequences remain. "God is not mocked, for whatever a man sows, that he will also reap." (Gal. 6:7.)

Illustrations of this fact with regard to the grosser sins are not hard to find. The drunkard abuses his family, his economic life, his health, and his total personality, and even if he does not die physically as a result, something dies within him as he loses his freedom to master his appetite. The lecherous person surrenders the joys of pure love and family life for a sensual and often short-lived pleasure. But such "death" is not limited to the sins of the flesh. The proud, arrogant, self-righteous person is so displeasing to others that he fails to receive, or to receive with any sincerity, the very plaudits that he covets most. The cold, hard, self-centered, yet outwardly respectable, person dies at the point of his capacity for unselfish concern for others, and as a consequence misses the richness of fellowship that is God's gift to those with more openness of soul. The sovereign God has so ordered His world that judgment is inescapable.

These things happen so generally, both to Christians and others, that they give some basis for a belief in automatic judgment. God does not vary either His physical or His moral laws to suit our pleasure. Yet we cannot suppose that God punishes through such consequences without great sorrow of heart and yearning to redeem us. The Christian understanding of judgment must never be divorced from redemption, or both will lose the all essential note of God's overarching, personal concern.

4. God's sovereignty in redemption

It is the chief cornerstone of Christian faith that Jesus Christ saves sinners. This theme has been dealt with at considerable length in the preceding chapter. I shall restate more briefly some of the things said there but in the context now of the relations of divine sovereignty to man's freedom in redemption through the grace of God.

What is grace? *It is the free, loving, personal activity of God in Christ for the salvation of undeserving man.* It presupposes repentance for sin and the willingness of sinful man in humility and trust to lay hold upon God's gift. Its correlate is the works which, though they cannot save, are the fruits of salvation. Grace costs much, both from God and man; yet it is free, for God imparts it graciously, spontaneously, naturally, without any coercion or restraint save that of His own nature.

If grace is the free, loving, personal activity of God in Christ for the salvation of undeserving men, we must look a little further at the meaning of these terms.

To say that grace is imparted *in love* is to affirm the basic insights of New Testament Christianity as epitomized in John 3:16. It connotes the willingness, even the yearning eagerness, of God to forgive the sinner and empower the weak. And grace can be neither free nor loving unless it is *personal*. In a person-to-person relation only are the conditions fulfilled by which it can be wrought. To say that it is the *activity* of God is to emphasize the social and dynamic character of the total relationship between God and man, not in redemption only but, as we have seen, in creation and judgment. To say that men are *undeserving* of such a free outpouring of God's mercy is to say what any sensitive soul

114

must recognize upon self-examination, if he is honest with himself.

Salvation "through Jesus Christ our Lord" lies at the heart of Christian faith. It is the meeting point of the creativity with the judgment of God; it is the key to the paradox of divine sovereignty and human freedom.

The God who is the Lord of all life takes the initiative in love. He discloses Himself, in a vision unsurpassed, to men who are formally free but spiritually bound. By this vision blind eyes are opened and dull hearts quickened to new life. In salvation through Christ revelation and redemption are so linked, the Vision and the Deed so at one, that no man having truly seen the vision can be free to act as if God had no claim upon him. He who has seen the Vision and felt the impact of the Deed is captive to it. Yet he is free—free with a new power to serve and honor him "in whose service is perfect freedom."

Thus, it comes about that the problems which most persistently vex men's minds, such as the relations of sovereignty to freedom and of God's omnipotence to his goodness in a world of pain and sin, become not *solved* but *resolved* by the Vision and the Deed. In a world in which we can be sure that God reigns, that Christ died for us and lives again, that He has given us His peace, we can accept the mystery and the gift and be of good cheer.

And this, after all, is just what the Christian means by the Eternal Goodness, coming to us in our human pilgrimage as the providence of God.

5. How does God overrule?

It has long been the deep conviction of Christian faith that God not only rules His universe and human affairs within it but that He *overrules* human decisions and shapes events according to His pleasure. This we find in the common, meaningful adage, "Man proposes but God disposes"; we find it again and again in the Bible. "A man's mind plans his way, but the Lord directs his steps," says a proverb far older than the one just quoted.[1]

[1] Prov. 16:9.

Never has the interplay of man's freedom with God's rule been put in more vivid juxtaposition than in Paul's word to the Philippians, ". . . Work out your own salvation with fear and trembling; for it is God at work in you, both to will and to work for his good pleasure" (Phil. 2:12-13).

From one angle this overruling of human wills is clear enough and has been presupposed in all that has thus far been said. No man's freedom is absolute; he must live his life, do his work, and make his choices within a structure of physical and moral laws which he did not make, but which God gives. At every turn reality imposes barriers to our flights of fancy, curbs our ambitions, slows us down, makes us turn around and go in some other direction than that which we had chosen. If in driving a car one comes to a dead-end street, he only smashes his car and himself if he tries to keep going forward, and it is the part of wisdom—and even of the most elementary common sense—to turn and go in another direction. This acceptance of limitations and redirection of goals is a major part of the business of living, and while we do not like to be thus inhibited, it is an essential mark of maturity to accept the inevitable without rebellion.

But this is not the whole issue, for this need to accept limitations imposed by forces stronger than one's own will can be viewed without reference to God simply as a matter of personal adjustment to circumstances. The heart of the matter from the standpoint of a doctrine of providence is (1) whether God imposes these limitations through a personal plan for the individual's life, and (2) whether God overrules for good even those evil circumstances which He does not will.

The answer to these queries, and in particular to the first, is tied in with the "God willing" which is the frequent proviso for a promise. We must now look at this more sharply.

As we look toward some anticipated event, is it legitimate to say that it will happen, "God willing?" And if we say it, do we mean that God's will is going to be done regardless of what human choices are made and acts performed by one's self or

116

another? The answer depends on the connotations attached to the words.

There are positive Christian values in *"Deus vult"* (God willing), or the abbreviated d.v., or the corresponding phrase in any language, provided we mean by it the subordination of the human spirit to the leading and providential care of the Ruler of all life. It ought to be accompanied by the thought, whether or not expressed in words, "I will try to discover and do the will of God for me in this situation, as fully as I can discern this will through the teaching of Christ and the voice of the Holy Spirit." On the contrary, if when we say "God willing" we mean to assert, "Whatever is going to happen will be right because nothing ever happens contrary to the will of God," then we are not affirming a true doctrine of the divine sovereignty but simply a doctrine of predestination. For reasons already given, providence does not mean predestination nor does the sovereignty of God require such a belief. What it does require is the confident faith that God cares for each of us, that He never forsakes us, that He wills the best possible in every human situation, and that He seeks to draw all men toward this goal.

The second question posed above, as to whether and how God overrules even evil events to bend them to His purpose, requires more reticence in the reply. Yet there is a sense in which it can be affirmed by the Christian that God makes even the wrath of men to praise Him.[2] This does not mean that He incites men to wrath in order to be praised; to assume this would make Him more like a demon than a god. It does mean that in spite of the worst that men may do to thwart His holy will, God is not defeated. Evil is self-defeating, as we noted earlier in reference to the penalties of sin, and individuals, groups, and nations that persist in ways that thwart God's will do so to their own destruction. Furthermore, both world history and individual experience give evidence that that which, upon its occurrence, looked like defeat and death has often in retrospect been life and hope.

[2] Cf. Ps. 76:10.

117

Israel's exile deepened her faith and gave her a deathless message; the shattering of the Roman Empire made way for Christianity; the defeat of Nazi Germany and of Japanese militarism in our own time would be attested by the Christians in those lands as a great step toward good. This is not to say that war is good, for it is the world's primary collective evil, but out of even this evil God is able to bring good into being.

When it is asked how God is able to overrule the evil of individual human lives for good, we are thrown back upon all that the Christian faith affirms as to God's redeeming grace. God does not will sin, but He wills victory over it and affords His grace through Jesus Christ for its conquest. Not all suffering is the will of God though obviously some forms of it are essential to personal growth to maturity. We are too finite to make any pontifical judgment as to just what suffering God does or does not will, though when it comes as the result of human sin, ignorance, or carelessness and crushes precious human values, we do well not to ascribe it to His purpose. Yet there is no suffering that God and man working together cannot turn to good. "We know that in everything God works for good with those who love Him." And it is at that third, middle ground kind of evil (frustration) that the work of God to bring good out of evil is most clearly evident in the imparting of new courage, direction, peace, and power.

The fruit of the Spirit in "love, joy, peace, patience, kindness, goodness, faithfulness, gentleness, self-control" becomes a visible witness to the power of God in transformed lives.

6. Divine foreknowledge

A final question remains to be raised as to the relation of God's sovereignty to our freedom, though it is one on which Christians will "agree to differ and resolve to love" in their replies.

Can we accept God's sovereign control over human acts and still preserve human freedom by a doctrine of divine foreknowledge? This is often urged as a way out of what otherwise appears to be an impasse, and in support of it the familiar words of Paul arc quotcd:

For those whom he foreknew he also predestined to be conformed to the image of his Son, in order that he might be the first-born among many brethren. And to those whom he predestined he also called; and those whom he called he also justified; and those whom he justified he also glorified.

(*Rom. 8:29-30.*)

The first thing to be said is that this passage is clearly related to a doctrine of divine election to salvation, but it does not bear upon the issue here under discussion, namely, God's foreknowing and hence foreordaining the particular events of daily life. If one holds to the latter, it must be on other grounds.

And, in the second place, to question the divine foreknowledge of free acts is not to impugn the infinite wisdom of God. Doubtless the God who has made us and who loves us does foresee the general course His human children are prone to take, whether as individuals or as the totality of the human race. It is unworthy of God to suppose that sin entered the world as any surprise to Him! Rather, He paid mankind the high tribute of creating us with freedom to follow His way or to defy it, and took the consequences. If a human parent who knows and loves his child can, in a measure, predict what this child will do under given circumstances, certainly God knows infinitely better. From this standpoint divine foreknowledge of the general pattern of human events is fully consistent with belief in His infinite wisdom, and the ejaculation often too lightly made, "Only God knows!" is not irrelevant.

But does God foreknow every event in which the free wills of men operate to affect the outcome? To the present writer it seems that there is inconsistency in affirming divine foreknowledge of genuinely free acts, not because God's wisdom is limited, but because freedom by its very nature involves some measure of unpredictable spontaneity. If either God or man knows in advance that a certain act will inevitably occur, can we call this act the result of a human decision freely made? I doubt it, for if freely made, the outcome *could* be otherwise. I shall not press the matter, for it is an issue on which it is not wise to claim to know more than we do know as to the mind of God. All that is essential is to maintain the reality of God's wisdom and man's free choices. Regardless of whether God foreknows in every instance how this freedom will be exercised, God has imparted it to us as an immeasurably precious gift and high responsibility.

The conclusion we arrive at after this examination of the relations of God's sovereignty to man's freedom is that both are real and always in conjunction. Shakespeare spoke truly when he wrote:

> There's a divinity that shapes our ends,
> Rough-hew them how we will.[3]

To deny either element implied in this couplet is to fall into error. There *is* a divinity that shapes our ends in spite of our roughhewing; yet we do far too much of it to fulfill the purpose of the Eternal Goodness. The meaning of providence is never so clear as when in the midst of sin, suffering, and frustration we sense the companionship of God and the lift of His redeeming grace.

[3] *Hamlet,* Act V, scene 2.

Chapter Six

PROVIDENCE AND PRAYER

WE COME NOW TO THAT WHICH, FROM A PRACTICAL STANDPOINT, is the heart of the question of providence. Does God hear and answer prayer? It is the testimony of the Bible and the all but unanimous witness of Christians that He does. But how does He answer it? And what sort of prayers does He answer? Here the difficulties become numerous, and the disparity of answers even among Christians of great sincerity becomes evident.

It is on this rock that many people's faith in providence is shipwrecked. On the one hand there are bitter experiences, such as that quoted in the introduction, when the most earnest prayers for the deliverance of a loved one from death or danger appear to fall on deaf ears, if any, and to bring no fruit. On the other there are many claims of "remarkable answers to prayer" that to sophisticated, to say nothing of skeptical, minds look like sheer coincidence in the occurrence of the events and self-deception in their interpretation. Even the person who is ready to say that God is the Creator is prone, almost without being aware of it, to fall into an implicit deism in which he assumes that while God made the world, natural laws govern it, and therefore, what is to happen will happen regardless of entreaty.

To get at this nest of problems, and so to find what assurances are credible, we must first ask what prayer is, then judge what we can believe God does in response to it.

1. What is prayer?

There is worship in every religion—a sense of reverence, homage, and praise before the Most High. Though the question of

121

what constitutes a religion, and in particular the question of whether there can be an atheistic religion, is a difficult one on which there is no full agreement, it is generally assumed that wherever there is religion there are also ritualistic acts. These rites not only reflect the devotion of the worshipers but the culture of the surrounding society, and as they are engaged in corporately, they serve to unite the community as well as to offer praise to its god or gods. Sometimes rites that are religious in their origin become mainly forms of secular tradition, as in the widespread observance of Shinto festivals throughout Japan and the too common secularization of Christmas, Easter, and Thanksgiving in America.[1]

Worship is expressed not only corporately but privately through both ritualistic acts and free, spontaneous expressions of praise and gratitude to God. As such it is basic to Christian prayer. We need not pause here to discuss corporate worship, since in most minds it forms no barrier to belief in providence, but it is essential to point out that without the mood of worship any prayer soon becomes barren and too easily passes over into self-centered importunity.

Prayer, as Christians understand the word, is not found in all religions, for prayer presupposes communication and response, and this can only be between Person and person. It is not prayer when we attempt to "rally the universe to our support," as the humanist might put it.[2] Christian prayer is prayer only when God meets man and man meets God in a living, personal encounter.

There is, perhaps, no fully inclusive definition of prayer, for it is the many-sided approach of the soul to God. However, the traditional words of the Westminster Shorter Catechism say it as well as it has ever been said. According to this, the answer to question 98 is as follows:

[1] The Shinto *torii* to most Americans means simply an artistic symbol of Japan, and I have seen it used, however inappropriately, for decorative effect in numerous Christian gatherings devoted to the study of Japan as a mission field.

[2] Cf. "A Humanistic Interpretation of Prayer" by John Haynes Holmes in *The Christian Century*, October 16, 1929.

Prayer is an offering up of our desires unto God, for things agreeable to his will, in the name of Christ, with confession of our sins, and thankful acknowledgment of his mercies.

Prayer is at least as much as this; it cannot be less. This statement has the advantage of stressing Christ-centeredness, our need of confession, and the impulse to thanksgiving. But it has also the particular value of putting petition in the right focus. Prayer *is* the expression of our desires—not some vague sort of musing or pleasant religion-tinctured feeling but the expression of our desires squarely in the focus of what is agreeable to God's will. Anything else becomes self-centered clamor and too easily degenerates into magical incantation or imprecation with the intent to have just what we want when we want it.

Prayer has many moods, as varied in their content as life itself. Paraphrasing Shelley, one might say of it, as of life, that it is "like a dome of many-colored glass," not so much staining the white radiance of eternity as affording the medium through which our stained souls are lifted up into the light of God's radiance that we may see more clearly both ourselves and His holy will.

Within these moods there are certain patterns, preferably not stereotypes, but certain basic elements. Every one of these, insofar as it is a legitimate part of Christian prayer, has some relation to providence. So let us now look at these in sequence. As we pray, they are often not in sequence but come flooding upon us and from us as a whole; yet we may consider them one by one to observe their meanings and implications.

To begin at the end of the definition cited above, prayer is "thankful acknowledgment of His (God's) mercies." Christian prayer rightly gets its orientation from the mood of thanksgiving, adoration, and praise, with these elements sometimes differentiated but more often blended in an act of worship in which the soul is lifted away from self and upward toward God. As an airplane cannot go anywhere except along its own runway until

123

it gets off the ground, neither can our prayers rise higher than ourselves unless we are willing and able to take elevation by a lift of the soul toward God in joyous thanksgiving.

And for what are we thankful? For a multitude of things, but basically "now thank we all our God" that He has led us along our way and even in adversity sustained us with blessings. And this is exactly what providence means! Virtually any hymn of praise will illustrate this truth, but I shall quote from one of the greatest, in which the convergence of thanksgiving with providence is clearly evident:

> Praise to the Lord, who o'er all things so wondrously reigneth,
> Shieldeth thee under His wings, yea, so gently sustaineth!
> Hast thou not seen how thy desires e'er have been
> Granted in what He ordaineth? [3]

Can one truly say that he can see how his desires have been granted in what God ordains? Then his desires are focused upon God and not upon his own ego; his petitions have become the offering up of his desires to God "for things agreeable to His will." In this mood providence is unquestioned; otherwise its reality tends to fade away and the best arguments to seem unconvincing.

To thank God prayerfully—and to pray thankfully—is to lift up to God a joyous sense of gratitude for His world and within it one's home, family, friends, work, play, health, "daily bread," and other material sustenance, the beauty of the world, the greatness and goodness of one's country, and much else. But it is also in a deeper sense to thank God for His supreme gift of grace in Jesus Christ and the continuing presence of the Holy Spirit in Christ's Church and in our lives. The English Book of Common Prayer puts this in true proportions and with incomparable dignity and beauty in its Prayer of General Thanksgiving:

[3] "Lobe den Herrn," By Joachim Neander, translated by Catherine Winkworth.

Almighty God, Father of all mercies, we, thine unworthy servants, do give thee most humble and hearty thanks for all thy goodness and loving-kindness to us, and to all men. We bless thee for our creation, preservation, and all the blessings of this life; but above all, for thine inestimable love in the redemption of the world by our Lord Jesus Christ; for the means of grace, and for the hope of glory.

When one can pray this prayer sincerely from the heart and through it thank God not only for His general goodness in creation but His particular "loving-kindness" in the guidance and sustaining of one's own life, then one believes in providence.

Yet this is a faith which, though it centers in God's free and gracious gift, must be earned by fitness to receive it. Not the fitness of merit but of obedient openness of spirit is the requirement. Accordingly the prayer continues with this petition:

And, we beseech thee, give us that due sense of all thy mercies, that our hearts may be unfeignedly thankful; and that we show forth thy praise, not only with our lips, but in our lives, by giving up our selves to thy service, and by walking before thee in holiness and righteousness all our days; through Jesus Christ our Lord, to whom, with thee and the Holy Ghost, be all honour and glory, world without end. AMEN.

It is not by accident that this prayer has been adapted for use by many churches other than that in whose liturgy it originally was formulated, for no words outside the Bible express more perfectly our faith in providence and the Christian's gratitude to the sovereign God who creates, redeems, and calls us to service.

Christian prayer includes also confession of our sins. This is a vital part of prayer that the petitioner sometimes forgets to include, but without it the petition is likely to get seriously out of focus.

Sin is in very ambiguous status in American Christian thought today, and this ambiguity affects our praying as well as living. It may, therefore, be helpful to add a few words to what was said about sin in Chapter Four.

125

Sin is a dominant and pervasive note in the Christian doctrine of man. In the older orthodoxy God's judgment upon sin, including the destiny of hell in store for the unforgiven sinner, was a controlling idea, and many a sermon centered in it. Usually in this context sin is conceived chiefly in its grosser manifestations of adultery, drunkenness, dishonesty, theft, and other forms of loose living and worldliness. The new orthodoxy, much more sophisticated and astute regarding both the subtler sins of the human heart and the prevalence of social sin, tends to make sin the keynote in its analysis of man's plight. In between these two types of orthodoxy, both historically and in the nature of its emphasis, stands liberalism.

Some liberals, and in particular those of an earlier day, have tended to underemphasize sin and hence have rightly evoked the criticism of both types of orthodoxy. It is still possible to find liberal churches in which the laymen and even the minister think of sin chiefly as infraction of the conventional moral patterns of the surrounding culture. Hence, being "good" people, they do not think of themselves as sinners! Yet the great liberals have never been so naïve. These words from one of them, deliberately selected from an old book to give evidence that the resurgence of a sense of sin in a chastened liberalism is no new phenomenon, put it this way:

The peril of sin as the innermost problem of human life is in these days obscure to many minds. . . . If a man, forgetting churches and sermons, seriously ponders human life as he knows it actually to be, if he gathers up in his imagination the deepest heartaches of the race, its worst diseases, its most hopeless miseries, its ruined childhood, its dissevered families, its fallen states, its devastated continents, he will soon see that the major cause of all this can be spelled with three letters—sin. . . . Sin is no bogey erected by the theologians, no ghost imagined by minds grown morbid with the fear of God. Sin to every seeing eye is the one most real and practical problem of mankind.[4]

[4] Harry Emerson Fosdick, The Meaning of Faith (New York and Cincinnati: Abingdon Press, 1917), p. 250-51.

If this be the case, as the wisdom both of the Bible and of current discernment gives evidence, there is a very large need in our praying for confession of sins. This ought not to be morbid self-excoriation. We must doubt that God is pleased by an ascetic flagellation of either body or spirit. Yet humble, honest, penitent, and *specific* acknowledgment of our sins, which are far more often sins of the spirit than of the flesh, is imperative. Contrition is the necessary condition both for God's forgiveness and our amendment of life. In great historic words which bring together creation and redemption and put both in the setting of contrition, we are told:

> For thus says the high and lofty One
> who inhabits eternity, whose name is Holy:
> I dwell in the high and holy place,
> and also with him who is of a contrite and humble
> spirit,
> to revive the spirit of the humble,
> and to revive the heart of the contrite.
> For I will not contend for ever,
> Nor will I always be angry;
> for from me proceeds the spirit,
> and I have made the breath of life.
> (Isa. 57:15-16)

The bearing of confession and penitence upon providence is perhaps not so obvious as is the relation of thanksgiving. Yet both from God's side and man's the connection is a vital one. The God who forgives and redeems by His unfailing grace is the God of eternal goodness who can always be trusted. No matter how terribly we may mar our destinies or those of others by sin, He stands ready to forgive the penitent and empower activity directed toward restitution and renewal. Without God the circumstances precipitated by sin in churned-up, individual lives and distorted social situations would often seem not only tragic but hopeless. With God there is always hope.

To seek God's forgiveness for past and present sin, and thus to find hope for the future, is an essential part of Christian prayer. To engage in prayer in this mood yields more faith in God's providence than can be established through any vindication of the ways of God that on speculative grounds alone tries to solve the problem of evil but overlooks the forgiveness of sin and the imparting of new life. "God shows his love for us in that while we were yet sinners, Christ died for us," (Rom. 5:8) and on this supreme showing of His love rests supremely our faith in His providential care.

This brings us to the basic note in prayer which ought to set the direction of all the rest—we pray "in the name of Christ." This is far more than the addition of the words "in Christ's name" or "through Jesus Christ our Lord" at the end of a prayer. Still less is it a magical formula to ensure getting what we ask for on the assumption that "ask what ye will in my name" brings guaranteed results.

To ask in the name of Christ is to ask in the spirit of Christ. It is to endeavor, as Jesus did, to make love for God and one another the dominant desire and motive of one's life; it is to trust, as Jesus did, in the loving, encompassing care of the Father. It is to direct our praying and our living toward "things agreeable to His will."

If one were to select one verse from the Bible which most aptly expresses what it means to pray in the name of Christ, it would be John 15:7: "If you abide in me, and my words abide in you, ask whatever you will, and it shall be done for you." Obviously, this cannot mean that every petition uttered by a Christian is bound to be answered as one desires! To make this assumption would put the manipulation of the universe into the hands of the pray-er, and this is magic, not religion. Furthermore, the facts of experience do not bear out this assumption. But if we put the emphasis where it ought to be laid—on the "if you abide in me . . . ," the whole situation becomes different. On that basis, then, we will not ask simply for the fulfillment of our own desires but for what God through Christ impels us to desire.

To pray in the name of Christ does not guarantee omniscience on our part as to what ought to be desired. Omniscience is reserved for God, not given to men. Many a time we must cry out as did Paul:

O the depth of the riches and wisdom and knowledge of God!
How unsearchable are his judgments and how inscrutable his ways!
"For who has known the mind of the Lord,
or who has been his counselor?" . . .
For from him and through him and to him are all things. To him be glory forever. (Rom. 11:33-36.)

Nevertheless, if we pray in the name and spirit of Christ, we can pray in trust of God's guiding and sustaining care, and thus, we can look with hope and confidence toward the future even in darkest days. The three things people need most today, both in private lives and in the world scene, are faith and hope and love. To pray in the name of Christ is to place ourselves in God's hands for their attainment.

We must now look carefully at a very large question or rather, two questions in one. For what can we pray in the name of Christ? And what efficacy can we expect our petitions to have? This double-barreled query requires a section of its own.

2. Types of petition

Petition, though it is not all there is of prayer, is central to it. Without thanksgiving and praise, confession and penitence, and a setting of our total approach to God in the framework of the revelation and redemptive work of God in Christ, petition, as has been noted repeatedly, is apt to get out of focus and become egocentric demand. Yet petition is not per se egocentric, and prayer, in the narrower sense of the word, is petition.

For what shall we make petition? Though in experience there need not and ought not to be any sharp delineation and systematizing of types of petition, fruitful analysis requires it. When

129

we pray, if the prayer is an outpouring of the whole soul before God and a receiving from God with the entire person, we do not categorize each petition with an (a), (b), or (c). Yet this does not prevent our *looking at* prayer with an (a), (b), (c) sequence. This we shall now proceed to do.

a) *Petitions for inner strength and renewal.* This is where the heart of petition lies, and one who believes in a prayer-hearing God at all will scarcely doubt the legitimacy and efficacy of prayer of this kind. It is the testimony of the ages that from this kind of prayer, entered into with sincerity and devotion, come inner peace, calmness, clarity of outlook, new strength, and efficiency for doing the task at hand. Illustrations of this fact in experience and literary expressions of it are too numerous to require extensive presentation. I shall cite two which are from different levels of religious experience but testify to the same great truth. The prophet Isaiah, proclaiming the sovereign God's creatorship and control over His world, had this to say also of God's personal helpfulness to those whose own strength is insufficient for life's demands:

> He gives power to the faint,
>   and to him who has no might he increases strength.
> Even youths shall faint and be weary,
>   and young men shall fall exhausted;
> but they who wait for the Lord shall renew their
>   strength,
>   they shall mount up with wings like eagles,
> they shall run and not be weary,
>   they shall walk and not faint.
>   (Isa. 40:29)

The frequency with which this passage is quoted gives evidence that it is not only one of the greatest in the Old Testament but that it speaks for and to the millions who feel beaten down, physically and nervously exhausted, and in need of more than they have.

The other passage I shall quote is from a gospel hymn, less often sung in "élite" churches now than formerly, but nevertheless full of power to speak for and to the human heart:

> Have we trials and temptations?
> Is there trouble anywhere?
> We should never be discouraged:
> Take it to the Lord in prayer.
> Can we find a friend so faithful
> Who will all our sorrows share?
> Jesus knows our every weakness:
> Take it to the Lord in prayer.[5]

The question at this point is not whether such prayer actually gives the comfort and support indicated in these two passages. The evidence is incontrovertible. Through prayer for inner strength and renewal, times without number have individuals found their weakness turned to strength, their anxiety to assurance, a baffled state of confusion transformed to clarity, and a sense of the ability to meet whatever may come. A new grip on life and a "second wind"—or integration of personality, acceptance, and adjustment if one prefers more psychological terms— is repeatedly observed as the fruit of prayer. Sometimes this has been recorded in terms of dramatic escape from danger through renewal of strength and insight, as in the late Rear Admiral Richard Byrd's witness to a sustaining Presence when he was sick, alone, and at the point of death in Antarctica, or James C. Whittaker's "There were other hands than mine on those oars," as superhuman strength was given him for deliverance from an imperilled life raft on the Pacific after three weeks of exposure and near starvation.[6] More often the fruit of prayer is found in the strength to endure calmly the demands of everyday living and

---

[5] From "What a Friend we have in Jesus" by Joseph Scriven (1820-86). It is found in innumerable hymn books and has been translated and sung throughout the world.

[6] Richard Byrd, *Alone*, and James C. Whittaker, *We Thought We Heard the Angels Sing*.

to meet life's minor as well as major crises with courage and hope.

For the skeptic the question is not whether this happens empirically but whether it happens *because of the believer's faith* rather than because of God—in a word whether such results are not subjectively induced. This suspicion lurks in not a few minds who would like to think otherwise and is a frontal challenge to Christianity from the unbeliever.

The answer does not lie simply in affirmation, for affirmation may be met by negative counter-declaration, and there is no meeting of minds. It lies rather in the total structure of positive grounds for belief in the personal God of Christian faith. Faith, indeed, is essential, and the persuasiveness with which the evidence presents itself will vary greatly according to the believer's own Christian experience. This is inevitable, since God is neither proved nor disproved on rational and scientific grounds. Yet there is not a little empirical evidence, which was outlined in Chapter Three, that the God of Christian faith exists. Transcending all of these facts is the revelation of God in Jesus Christ to give meaning and assurance to such indices from other sources. Whether one believes that God *does anything in* prayer hinges on the answer to a much larger question, namely, whether one believes that God *does anything.*

If this larger question is answered in the affirmative, the psychological or subjective aspects of prayer become ways in which God works in cooperation with the human spirit. There need then be no hesitancy to affirm that the believer's faith in a prayer-hearing and prayer-answering God gives steadiness to the nerves, broadens and clarifies perspective, turns the introvert's attention outward, and directs the extrovert's gaze inward toward a needed self-analysis. Doubtless even one's adrenal glands are affected by prayer, and this may well be one way in which "they who wait for the Lord" find their strength renewed. Yet this is a long way removed from saying that prayer is "nothing but" autosuggestion resulting in such psychological and even physical changes. The

God who creates and sustains human life and personality re-creates and supports us through processes psychologically discernible; yet it is He and not our own imaginings that does it. If the God of Christian faith exists—and whether He does is an ultimate choice to be determined by the evidence apprehended in faith—then He answers prayers for inward strength and renewal. The words reported as spoken by King David to his son Solomon may well be taken as spoken to us but with the deeper meaning and confidence that comes from praying "in the name of Christ":

And you, Solomon my son, know the God of your father, and serve him with a whole heart and with a willing mind; for the Lord searches all hearts, and understands every plan and thought. If you seek him, he will be found by you. (*I Chr.* 28:9.)

b) *Petitions for physical health and healing.* We shall defer for the present the question of the efficacy of prayer for the health of others, since this is a matter of intercessory prayer which has problems and possibilities of its own. How far, then, may we believe that prayer affects the state of one's body as well as spirit?

It must be said at the outset that there is less certainty at this point than in reference to petition for inner strength and spiritual renewal. Caution, therefore, is in order at the point of claiming to know more than we do. Yet caution ought not to be invoked to oppose an affirmative and defensible faith in spiritual healing.

One of the most significant changes that have come over medical practice in recent years is the recognition that a person is the whole person, not bone, blood, glands, and cellular tissue only, and that both illness and health are matters of the whole person in which attitudes of mind and spirit play a very important part. One physician of unquestioned competence writes:

In the course of the last thirty years an increasing number of physicians and laymen have accepted the concept that illness of mind and body can be caused by psychological influences and that they

133

can be treated successfully by psychologic methods. Much of this development is recognized nowadays as scientifically well founded because the findings satisfied two crucial criteria: they occurred often enough to be *statistically significant* and the observations could be *repeated experimentally* in hospital or laboratory.[7]

This healing of body and mind together is what is ordinarily called psychosomatic medicine. It is not exactly the same thing as spiritual healing or what has long been called "faith healing," for neither the doctor nor the patient need be a religious person in order to have these results occur. Faith, indeed, is necessary, but it may be faith in the physician or the psychiatrist or the sick person's faith in his own recuperative powers that brings about the desired result.

Spiritual healing is recovery wrought by the power of God. By its very nature it is less open to statistical investigation and scientific analysis. Because God's way with men is always in some measure a mystery, reticence is in order as to saying just how or to what extent God heals in response to prayer. Yet there is no presumption in holding that God heals at *least* through psychosomatic as well as through directly physical processes. That there is a *plus* beyond this we may well believe; there is certainly not a *minus*. To one who believes that God works throughout His world "to will and to do His good pleasure," there is no inconsistency in supposing that He uses the laws both of body and spirit to help and to heal in response to prayer.

Another physician in an article in *The Christian Century* has spelled this out with great clarity. In "Prayer Helps Maintain Health" Dr. Donald M. Robertson shows how in neurotic tension the blood distribution is upset and emergency body mechanisms which were given us as protection against sudden threats become overworked. High blood pressure and a strain on the

---

[7] Gotthard Booth, M.D., *Healing: Human and Divine* (ed. Simon Doniger; New York: Association Press, 1957), p. 217. Dr. Booth is associated with the Columbia University Seminar on Religion and Health and is psychiatric adviser to Union Theological Seminary and the General Theological Seminary.

circulatory system are results. But this is not all. So far reaching are the effects on many organs of the body that his analysis is worth quoting:

Various kinds of malfunction and subfunction result. The glands of internal and external secretion are thrown out of normal balance. Digestion becomes inadequate, and this state of affairs can lead to malfunction, then disease, of the digestive tract. Ulcers, colitis, indigestion, constipation and gall-bladder disease may be the results of such faulty functioning. The glands controlling metabolism are often stimulated, leading to thyroid malfunction and even to goiter. The reproductive organs are depressed in function, a condition leading to sterility and impotence and all sorts of functional menstrual disorders. Nervous perspiration with its peculiar chemical content, odor and color is increased, often to the embarrassment of the individual.[8]

In addition to such bodily effects neurosis is cumulative, leading to more and more tension, sleeplessness, depression, and fatigue. The individual's behavior becomes compulsive and defensive; egocentricity is deepened; feeling-states of suspicion, jealousy, hate, fear, anxiety, and distrust breed other feeling-states of frustration, loneliness, and a sense of being rejected and unwanted.

It is apparent that this state of affairs, in greater or less degree, is widely prevalent in our time. It may not lead to death or insanity, though it may; it is certain to cause acute unhappiness and the loss of effective living. And it need not be so.

Dr. Robertson is a physician, not a theologian. Yet no theologian could put the answer more clearly or more aptly than he does. So let us listen to him again:

It is only when we began to grow from self-centeredness into God-centeredness, from egocentricity to theocentricity, that we can over-

[8] Issue of January 16, 1957. Copyright 1957 Christian Century Foundation. Reprinted by permission from The Christian Century. Reprints of this article are available from the office of The Christian Century, 407 So. Dearborn St., Chicago, Ill.

135

come neurotic patterns of behavior and replace them with mature and adult patterns. Only when we fit ourselves into God's plans for us and his creation are we able to see ourselves as we really are and our fellow men as brothers sharing a common Father in a common universe. . . .

In other words, prayer promotes maturity and eliminates neuroses and neurotic behavior. That is why I as a physician assign such an important place to prayer in relationship to this problem of health. Repeated God-centering of our lives gradually dispels harmful negative emotions, breaks down the fences which keep God out, and replaces them with faith, hope, love, acceptance, trust and confidence. This leads to a feeling-state of belonging, of being needed and wanted, of having purpose in this world and in God's plan for it. It gives that ultimate security which comes only from surrendering our lives completely to God, putting our destiny in his hands.

Then the old physical machine can turn off its defenses, the watchdogs can be called off. Blood pressure drops, digestion is re-established, tensions dissolve and normal sleep returns. So we will begin to experience growing health.[9]

I have quoted at length from this statement by a scientifically trained Christian layman because it says so much, not only about prayer but about providence. The only thing that need further be said about spiritual healing is a word both of affirmation and of caution.

The Bible again and again records incidents of spiritual healing, not only in the miracles wrought by Jesus but in the early Church. Furthermore, the practice of spiritual healing has never been absent from the Church. Though it is unnecessary to take at face value all that has been claimed in the name of faith healing, there have been miracles at Lourdes, healings by Christian Science, and recovery of health by ordinary Protestants in response to prayer that are unexplainable on any other grounds and are too well authenticated to be lightly dismissed. The question is not so much whether spiritual healing occurs as to what should be one's expectation in regard to it.

[9] *Ibid.*

Here the warnings are to be entered. Spiritual healing should never be made a substitute for medical care. There is something deeply tragic, and we may well believe it to cause great sorrow to the heart of God, when a preventable death occurs through trusting to faith alone and rejecting scientific skill. Although the power of life and death is ultimately in God's hands, not ours, he has made us stewards of it, and it is almost blasphemy to attribute to "the mysterious dispensation of Providence" a death which could have been prevented by wise human action.

Second, the power to heal is itself a sacred trust to be used in stewardship to God. Apart from the medical and surgical skills acquired by long training, some individuals appear to be endowed with charismatic gifts of healing. Such powers of healing through faith as are witnessed to in Agnes Sanford's *The Healing Light* ought not to be disparaged but inquired into with open minds. If God has granted to one's hands this power to heal, the committed Christian will not commercialize it or use it for self-advertising or self-exaltation; he will use it humbly and gratefully for human good.

And, in the third place, one's faith in God ought never to stand or fall with the outcome of a particular prayer for health. It is obvious that not every prayer for recovery is answered in the affirmative. The evidence appears to be that the healing of organic diseases by prayer alone occurs very rarely and is certainly less common than in circumstances where there is a combination of sound medical treatment with a calm and ordered mind.

When such healing does occur, is it a miracle? That is a large question to be examined in another chapter. But of this we can be confident, that God wills for each of us the best that can be had under our particular circumstances. In the pursuit and finding of this best both prayer and human effort are indispensable.

c) *Petitions in regard to natural events.* We have for some pages been considering a natural event of great importance— the recovery from sickness of the human body. Yet so intertwined are body and spirit in the total personality that what happens to the body is never wholly a physical matter.

137

The clearest case of a natural event is the weather, with its sunshine and storms, its rain, snow and ice, its winds which may vary from the gentlest of zephyrs to destructive hurricanes and tornadoes. Along with the weather and the earthquakes and floods before which man often appears helpless, there is a vast range of hazardous encounter between men and machines, ranging from industrial machinery through automobiles and airplanes to implements of terrible military destructiveness. And there is all the while the danger of fire, of drowning, of the power of gravitation to crush the human body when it falls or when other objects fall upon it, and many other ways in which death or accident comes suddenly upon us. No wonder it is a natural impulse of the human spirit to pray for deliverance from danger!

At no other point do we need to be so guarded in declaring what we may or may not expect God to do in response to prayer. But let us look at the issues.

First, let it be clear that the entire natural order is God's order. It is not something that stands over against Him as an enemy, sometimes pleasing, often thwarting Him. It is not something self-caused and independent which God is trying to coax into submission. Nor is it something, as the deist might hold, once made by God but then left to run itself, as one might wind up a watch or an automatic toy. This world is God's world; nature's laws are God's laws, and He is everywhere present in His world.

And, in the second place, God does not deviate from His orderly ways of working in response simply to human desire, though within these orderly ways events of great importance to men occur. Life is not all hazardous; nature is the very framework of our living and the scene of great satisfactions. Without such order to be counted on, life would be far more hazardous and far less satisfying than it is. We cannot have it both ways, and danger is a price we pay for the orderliness of nature.

The third thing, crucial to any understanding of prayer within this field, is that God uses nature to express and to fulfill His high purposes for men. Nature, though orderly, is not a closed

138

system into which nothing new can come. Man, certainly, can discover and use the laws of nature to bring about great changes in natural events. All securing of "our daily bread" and of much beyond the bare necessities of life is through such use of nature to fulfill human purposes. What man can do, and so obviously does do, it is irrational to suppose God cannot do.

We do well, therefore, to continue to pray for safety and for human welfare of all sorts within the natural world. Yet we do well also to continue to work for it and not to expect God to shift the structure of His universe in our behalf. Dr. Buttrick puts the paradox in these words:

There are fixities of faithfulness in God's nature: science calls them "law." But there are surprises in God's nature by which "he sets in at single points"; religion calls them His very word and deed. He is adamant Truth and intimate Love—never-changing and ever-changing Life.[10]

Not all our petitions are granted. Says the same author, "Not all our praying will change the position of the planet Neptune, or make winter follow spring, or cause a new arm to sprout at the place of amputation." [11] Yet things do happen in response to prayer—more "than this world dreams of." Most often these desired changes in natural events occur in conjunction with human effort, as when dams or dykes are built, flood control measures instituted, safety appliances put in machinery, brakes tightened, precautionary measures taught to children and adults, persons stirred to help one another. Life, though precarious, has no need to be appalling. Yet beyond these measures, in which our prayers may well impel us to more responsible human action, lies the area in which God acts for our protection and well-being. There is no barrier in logic to the belief that the same God who has made our world and is present in it can control even the weather in response to His wise purposes. It is the part of human wisdom to pray for daily bread, for safety, and for the enhance-

[10] *Prayer* (New York and Nashville: Abingdon Press, 1942), p. 92.
[11] *Ibid.*, p. 94.

ment of the conditions of human happiness, meanwhile continuing to labor toward these ends and leaving with God the outcome.

3. Prayer for others

One area of great importance remains to be spoken of, which traditionally and to the present has been called intercessory prayer, though simply "prayer for others" is more aptly descriptive. Intercession, if one wishes to be literal as to the word, suggests that God is being asked to change His mind, and this we can hardly think to be a correct meaning of the term.

To many minds, prayer for others, if carried beyond its obvious effects in making one individual more sensitive to the needs of another and thus more prone to help him, is an enigma. It appears on the face of it to do what has just been suggested as an undesirable connotation, namely, to try to persuade God to alter His chosen ways. It might be an unwarranted impingement on the other's freedom. It seems to imply changes in another's state without any direct communication, and when the analogy of mental telepathy or some other form of parapsychology is invoked to give it scientific credence, this cheapens its spiritual meaning. Furthermore, if the effects are *only* those of telepathic communication, evil thoughts as well as good can be transferred, and we are dangerously close to incantation!

Looking squarely at these difficulties, as we must if we are to be honest, what of the Christian's agelong, intuitive prompting to pray for those he loves and desires to help?

That it is an intuitive, deep-seated prompting of the human spirit is hardly to be denied. "A blasphemer will cry out for himself in physical or moral disaster, 'Oh, God!' That cry is not mere blasphemy; he must call on something beyond the human, and the word 'God' best answers his need." [12] Yet beyond this out-

[12] *Ibid.*, p. 100.

cry, which may be half-profane, half-seeking, and wholly self-centered, there are very few mature persons who have not felt at one time or another impelled to pray for those they love. Even though they must hope against hope, still men pray in times of crisis for those with whom their lives are knit. That it is a characteristic human impulse does not prove its validity, but it does indicate its naturalness and its importance.

But we must go deeper. The prayers of Jesus give us our pattern, and when we look to the example of Jesus, we find him praying for others again and again. In addition to his great, high priestly prayer at the Last Supper where intercession reaches its climax in the prayer that his followers may all be one,[13] we find him praying during his ministry for the people about him, for Peter that his faith fail not,[14] for little children,[15] for his enemies on the cross.[16] He urged his followers to "pray for those who persecute you" [17] and to pray that laborers be sent forth into the harvest.[18] Christians through many centuries have followed both the example and the behest of their Lord in praying for others and have believed that their prayers were answered. Without such prayer Christian faith would lose much of its richness and power.

Some things we can say with certainty as to the ways in which such prayers are answered. At other points we must leave it to Infinite Wisdom to do more than our poor analyses can fathom or demonstrate. At the least some obstacles can be cleared away.

It is certain that when we pray, not perfunctorily but vitally and with great depths of concern for those prayed for, a new sensitiveness to their need emerges in us, and we see more clearly what we ought to do and can do to help them. A new situation

[13] John 17.
[14] Luke 22:32.
[15] Matt. 19:13.
[16] Luke 23:34.
[17] Matt. 5:44; Luke 6:27.
[18] Matt. 9:38; Luke 10:2.

141

in the heart is created, and out of the heart are the issues of life, whether the matter be ministry to another in his sin or suffering, the giving of "a cup of cold water" in Christ's name, or service to the peace of the world. It is certain also that when others know that they are being prayed for, a sense of being upborne by the prayers of friends and loved ones gives added strength and courage.

These certainties ought not to be disparaged, for they are of great significance. It may well be that God has ordained that these changes in the pray-er and the prayed for should be His primary mode of response. Yet they do not answer what is the heart of the problem for many, namely, *whether God does anything* when we pray for others. In a word the question is whether our prayers in any way influence God and through His action thereby influence the results.

One is apt at first glance to recoil from the idea that we in any way influence God. Yet if God is personal, every prayer for forgiveness and indeed every prayer of communion and fellowship is a personal encounter. Says a wise contemporary theologian:

But if prayer is communication with God it implies the exerting of an effect on God. If God is not aware that I am addressing him, then my attempt at communication has failed. If he is aware, then God himself is having an experience which he would not have had without my having prayed; in short my prayer has had an effect upon him.[19]

This is not to say that my praying changes God's mind as to what is best for another or bends His will to match mine. It does mean that, whether I pray for myself or for another, my prayer is meaningful to God. It clearly helps to open blocked channels in me; may it not also be used by Him to open channels of grace

[19] L. Harold DeWolf in "The Influence of Prayer on God and Man," in *Healing: Human and Divine*, p. 146.

into another's life? We cannot suppose that God forces His blessings upon another against the other's will, so sacred is the freedom God has endowed us with. Yet there is no final barrier to the belief that when we pray, God uses not only our direct service but our prayers in helpfulness to others. Indeed, so knit together are we potentially in "one great fellowship of love throughout the whole wide earth" that in praying for others this potentiality becomes reality and prayer becomes a form of service in which God uses this devotion of the heart. *How* He does it we do not fully know; *that* He does it is consistent with everything else in our Christian faith.

As in the case of petition for ourselves, not every prayer for others is answered as we wish, or even as we think it ought to be in accordance with what we know of the will of God. Loved ones prayed for die; sons prayed for in wartime are killed in battle; even those whose conversion we earnestly pray for do not always respond. It is no service to true religion to evade this grim fact. We live in an infinitely complex world wherein prayer is not the only factor for God or man to reckon with. Yet again and again we *can* see answers to our prayers for others, and without having to dub the circumstance "coincidence," we can gratefully give thanks. Knowing by faith God's loving concern, we shall keep on praying.

The basic fact about both petition for ourselves and prayer for others is the new spiritual situation it creates, the greater outreach of the human heart to God, the closer fellowship of man with man and of man with God in the ties of personal communion thereby made more binding. Outside the Bible this has never been said better than in certain familiar words of Tennyson. With these we bring this chapter to a close:

> More things are wrought by prayer
> Than this world dreams of. Wherefore, let thy voice
> Rise like a fountain for me night and day.
> For what are men better than sheep or goats

That nourish a blind life within the brain,
If, knowing God, they lift not hands of prayer
Both for themselves and those who call them friend?
For so the whole round earth is every way
Bound by gold chains about the feet of God.[20]

[20] "The Passing of Arthur" in *Idylls of the King*, ll. 415 ff.

144

Chapter Seven

MIRACLE AND NATURAL LAW

FROM TIME TO TIME IN EARLIER CHAPTERS THE QUESTION OF miracle has been touched upon, with the promise to deal with it more specifically in a later chapter. We have now arrived at this point. So complex is the whole matter of miracles, whether thought of in their biblical setting or as occurring in the contemporary world, that almost anything that can be said is easily open to misunderstanding. Yet so intimately related is this matter to faith in providence that it must be looked at squarely and without evasion.

To some minds the literal accuracy of every miracle story in the Bible, from the floating of the axe head in the story of Elisha,[1] through Jonah's submarine journey,[2] to the virgin birth of Jesus,[3] appears so essential that to doubt one of them is not only to doubt the Bible but to doubt God Himself. A whimsical reference even to such dramatic incidents as Noah and his ark or Daniel in the lion's den arouses hurt, suspicion, and even anger. On the other hand to large numbers of our contemporaries such miracle stories of the Bible as have become known through the thick veil of the prevalent biblical illiteracy seem simply to be "tall tales," interesting but certainly primitive ways of telling what no intelligent person today could think credible. With this point of view goes usually an attempt to substitute science for miracle in modern life.

Somewhere in between these two attitudes the truth pre-

[1] II Kings 6:5-7.
[2] Jonah 1:17; 2:10.
[3] Matt. 1:18-25; Luke 1:26-35; 2:4-7.

145

sumably lies. It is our task now, if not to locate it precisely, to give a frame of reference for its location.

1. What is a miracle?

The difficulty does not lie exclusively in biblical interpretation, though this in itself is a large matter, but in something deeper. Whether we are speaking of the biblical miracles, those believed to have been wrought in the history of the Church through the Virgin or the saints, or the miracles of today, there is difference of opinion as to what a miracle is.

Sometimes the term miracle is used in a loose and general sense simply to indicate something strange or unusual or not expected. If one loses the proverbial "needle in a haystack" and finds it again, the finding of it is deemed a miracle! More often, however, a miracle is taken to mean a suspension or violation of a law of nature. Most things happen on the basis of an encompassing natural order within which causes and effects can be traced; some things seem not to have any natural cause and these are deemed supernatural and hence miraculous events. This view presupposes a system of nature open to scientific analysis, with miracles as interventions. Yet this is not what miracle means in the Bible, for in Bible times there was no scientific concept of an unvarying natural order to serve as a backdrop to the idea, and it is by no means certain that this is what miracle ought to mean today.

Harry Emerson Fosdick, in a chapter entitled "Miracle and Law" in his *Modern Use of the Bible*, has given a helpful delineation of the historical stages through which the idea of miracle has passed. In primitive animistic society everything not done by man is thought to be done by an extrahuman spirit and thus to be miraculous. The Bible, though without any framework of exact natural law, assumes that all nature is the sphere of God's activity. Within it there are great regularities, as in the promise that follows the story of the flood, "While the earth remains, seedtime and harvest, cold and heat, summer and winter, day and night, shall not cease" (Gen. 8:22). But there are also occasions on which God chooses to work in other than His ordinary ways, and these are miracles. The next stage of development was that in which the medieval church, influenced by the Greek idea of a cosmic order, came to regard miracles as interventions in this order. This concept was carried over into modern times with the idea of inflexible, unvarying natural law as the basis of all science. On this foundation miracles are commonly believed either not to occur at all or to occur only by a special divine intervention. The implicit assumption, which we must note carefully is that of the philosophic system known as deism rather than of biblical thought, is that God has created the world but left it to run by itself except as He may choose to intervene and temporarily make it behave in some extraordinary way. When this occurs, there is thought to be a suspension of a law of nature.

This idea of intervention is implicit in most current thought about miracles. Not only are there the "acts of God" like the floods, hurricanes, and earthquakes referred to in the insurance policies, in which God is assumed to intervene in nature to do damage, but whenever there is an unexpected escape from danger, an unexpected turn of good fortune, we are likely to call this a miracle. As I shall attempt to show presently, there may be good reason for deeming such an event a miracle, and certainly we ought gratefully to thank God for it. But what we ought *not* to do is to assume that God was absent from the normal, ordinary developments of life and present only in the unexpected.

What, then, is a miracle? We may get at its meaning helpfully from its derivation in the Latin *miror, mirari,* to wonder. Those readers who studied Vergil's *Aeneid* in high school will recall the frequency with which the words *mirabile dictu* occur. "Wonderful to relate"—that is an essential ingredient of miracle! Yet a miracle is more than something *mirabile*, something amazing on the human plane and to man's expectancy. It is this, but *miraculum* in the religious sense means something wonderful that God has done. In short miracles are God's wonderful works,

147

which call forth in us amazement, gratitude, and a deep sense of reverence before a Power that is not man's or nature's only, but God's.

Are all of God's wonderful works to be deemed miracles? In a sense they are, for the wonders of the natural universe which science increasingly discloses, like the more familiar facts of the marvelous symmetry and individuality of the snow crystal, the growth of a minute seed to flower or shrub or tree, the infinite variety of human personalities in God's world, are facts to evoke in the sensitive religious spirit a feeling of awe and wonder. "What hath God wrought!" was not only an appropriate message to cross the Atlantic in the first cabled communication a century ago, but it ought often to be in the heart and on the lips of the Christian. There is no need to exclude the daily events and familiar facts of life from the realm of the miraculous, provided these are thought of as the work of God and their occurrence calls forth a sense of wonder, praise, and gratitude.

Miracles in this sense correspond to and are an important aspect of general providence. Yet the term miracle is more often used, and may be properly used, in a narrower sense which has its correlate in special providences. It is here that Herbert H. Farmer finds the primary focus of its meaning. He points out that it is at a time of critical need, when we have prayed to God for help and feel overwhelmingly a sense of succour from Him, that we are most likely to speak of the event as a miracle. "The principle upon which this focalisation of meaning takes place is that *the more intensely personal and individual the succour of God is felt to be, the more appropriate and inevitable the word miracle becomes on the religious man's lips.*" [4] Miracle then becomes both a revelation of God's personal love and care and a saving act. It is not simply the startling, unexpected character of the event that makes it a miracle but the degree of poignancy with which it demonstrates God's providential care of the individual in his need.

[4] Farmer, *op. cit.*, p. 118. Italics his.

There is no necessity to choose between miracle in these two senses. Each reinforces and gives meaning to the other. Though all of life bespeaks the wonder of God's works to the listening ear, special evidences of God's providential care occasionally appear, so striking and arresting that we are jarred out of our customary acquiescence in things as they are and sent to our knees in gratitude. An unexpected recovery of health, whether of ourselves or those we love, a remarkable escape from danger, an extraordinary blessing of any type may be so regarded, though the greatest miracle of all is to become "a new creation" in Christ. When the new depth of feeling thus elicited surges over the soul, then the presence of God in all of life becomes more vivid and meaningful. Yet it is equally true, as has earlier been stated, that special providences occur *within* a structure of general providence, not outside it or at variance with it.

It is not the strangeness of an occurrence or even our failure to understand it that makes an event a miracle. The tricks of the magician or sleight-of-hand artist are not miracles and are seldom so regarded. There is a sense in which Augustine was right when he wrote, "A miracle (portentum) is not contrary to nature, but to what is known as nature." [5] In every miracle there is an element of marvel and surprise, and since familiarity tends to dull the sense of wonder, we do not usually speak of everyday events as miracles. Yet the distinctive note in miracle is not the frequency or rarity of its occurrence, but what God is doing through it. It is when with a gripping clarity we see God at work in His world, and in particular, out of a deep spiritual need we see Him at work for us, that miracle becomes real.

It is apparent, therefore, that miracle is essentially a religious category, not a philosophical or scientific one. This is not to say that it is irrelevant to philosophy or science. If it were, this chapter would not need to be written. Nevertheless, the final mean-

[5] Augustine, *De Civitate Dei*, Bk. XXI, viii.

ing of miracle is not to be settled by its relation to natural law; its meaning centers in the relation of God as personal, loving Spirit to human lives.

To revert to Fosdick's discussion of miracle, he has given a definition that with a little shift of emphasis seems to me admirable. "A miracle," he says, "is God's use of his own law-abiding powers to work out in ways surprising to us his will for our lives and for the world." [6] Written in 1924 when the eagerness of Christian liberalism to come to working relations with natural science was at its height, these words perhaps stress unduly the "law-abiding" powers of God, as if the God who had made the laws must be subject to them. Yet taken in conjunction with the author's qualifying propositions, this is a long way from making God's action rigidly mechanical. These are: (1) that the concept of "law" does not exhaust reality, (2) that law is not a means of imprisonment to personality, but of release, and (3) that existence is not a closed system into which nothing new can come.[7] These propositions will become very relevant as we look presently at the meaning of natural law.

It should by now be apparent to the reader that I have a high regard for the concept of miracle but reject the idea of divine intervention.

God does not have to come in from the outside of our world in order to act; the transcendent yet always immanent God is here. He acts constantly, creating new elements in our world, sustaining and directing the total process, bringing personal help to the individual in his deepest need. Every element in nature is God's; every natural law is God's law; the presence of God as Supernature is throughout all nature. There is no need, therefore, to distinguish between miracles as "supernatural" phenomena and the wonders of God's world. Yet this is not to deny that miracles occur or to attempt to run everything under

---

[6] *The Modern Use of the Bible* (New York: Association Press, 1924), p. 162.
[7] *Ibid.*, pp. 158-61.

150

an inflexible "reign of law." This prompts us to inquire next what is meant by natural law.

2. What is natural law?

By a law of nature is meant the formulation of an observed regularity in natural events. The principal object of pure science, often called descriptive science to distinguish it from technology and other forms of applied science, is to discover and formulate the manifold aspects of regularity among the phenomena of nature. In some fields there must be experimentation under rigidly controlled conditions; in all fields open to scientific investigation there must be accurate, and if possible, often repeated observations. What is discovered to be the normal characteristic or type of behavior of the object under investigation is then formulated as a law. Where possible such laws are expressed in mathematical formulae, as in physics and chemistry; where there are general trends within which individual variations occur, as in the biological and social sciences, the laws take the form of statistical averages.

The newer trends in physics, particularly the quantum theory, tend to question a fixed uniformity even in the physical world. Classical mechanics held to a complete and thoroughgoing determinism. The Heisenberg *principle of indeterminacy* challenges this assumption.

There is a universal indeterminacy measured by a universal constant of nature . . . to which all objects are subject regardless of their nature. For very small objects such as an electron or an atom, this indeterminacy becomes decisive and makes it impossible to specify both their position and their velocity simultaneously with precision. If either one is precisely known, then the other will be wholly indeterminate. . . .

The purpose of any theory is to represent faithfully the world as it actually is constituted. . . . Whether we like it or not, it seems to be a world in which indeterminacy, alternative, and chance are real aspects of the fundamental nature of things, and not merely the consequence of our inadequate and provisional understanding.[8]

The above assertion is from the same author quoted earlier on the dependable regularities of nature—an atomic physicist who is also an ordained minister and therefore unusually qualified to speak in both fields. To his thought-provoking book the reader is referred for the deductions which he draws from the actuality of chance, which he believes makes legitimate a doctrine of providence fully compatible with the principles of science.

The procedure I follow is not dependent on quantum physics, in which I have no competence. I believe, however, that the newer physics is extremely important from one angle and dangerously deceptive from another in regard to the Christian's faith in miracle and providence. It is important in refutation of a rigidly mechanical interpretation of nature. What Dr. Pollard calls chance I should prefer to call spontaneity or flexibility or simply the possibility of alternatives, and this is consistent with the conviction of Christian faith that ours is an orderly and dependable but not a mechanically determined world. On the other hand there is an easy temptation to defend faith by overstressing flexibility and hence understressing the reality of cause and effect relations. Within these our lives are set, and we must reckon with them.

No one needs to be told that the scientific discovery and formulation of the laws of nature hold an enormously important place in modern life. Scientific research on a vast scale centers at this point. Thus an increasingly complex body of knowledge is being acquired in many fields, on the basis of which not only the understanding of relations among events is possible but to a high degree also their prediction, control, and utilization to satisfy man's desires. The conquest of many forms of disease, technological expansion, the fission of the atom, and now the conquest of outer space by the launching of man-made satellites are the results of a scientific discovery of nature's laws.

[8] Pollard, op. cit., pp. 53, 54-55.

By a curious misconception, of which no real scientist is guilty but which too often crops up in popular discussion, it is assumed that natural laws have some sort of causal efficacy. Yet obviously *the laws* do nothing; they simply describe what is done. The crux of the matter lies in the fact that there are two kinds of explanations, both real in their own context but often confused. There is scientific or phenomenal explanation which traces the sequences of cause and effect which have been formulated as laws; there is ultimate or ontological explanation which is concerned with the source, meaning, and goal of all that is. Science moves in the first realm; philosophy and theology in the second. Both are aspects of existence, and are not in conflict if rightly understood, but they ought never to be confused with each other or substituted for each other.

To take a simple illustration, it is obvious to anybody that a sufficient drop in temperature turns water to ice, as a rise in temperature turns it to steam. The conditions under which this occurs with variations according to atmospheric pressure are part of the science of physics, and the relations of heat to mechanical power a matter of thermodynamics. Ordinarily in talking about ice and steam we do not stop to say that God is doing the freezing and melting, though in a worshipful mood one may say with the psalmist:

> He sends forth his command to the earth;
>   his word runs swiftly.
> He gives snow like wool;
>   he scatters hoarfrost like ashes.
> He casts forth his ice like morsels;
>   who can stand before his cold?
> He sends forth his word, and melts them;
>   he makes his wind blow, and the waters flow.
> (Ps. 147:15-18)

If we keep the two kinds of causality in proper relations, it is correct enough to say that natural forces cause events to happen, the course of which under known conditions can be traced in

153

retrospect and predicted with considerable accuracy. This is what science is doing all the time, and on the basis of such observed regularities an amazing body of scientific knowledge has been accumulated. However, it is not correct to set nature and God over against each other, as if nature did some things and God did others. *All the laws of nature are God's laws.* The chief error in the intervention concept of miracle arises from disregard of this all-important fact.

Nor is this all. Natural laws describe what happens normally and regularly; it is their function to describe "observed uniformities" in nature when no conflicting circumstances are present. Yet in the real world circumstances of almost infinite complexity keep impinging on one another all the time. That is why it is necessary to isolate a disease germ or any other phenomenon that may be under investigation in order to get accurate knowledge of it. Natural laws are abstractions, stating what would happen ideally or under rigidly controlled conditions, not what happens actually under the complex set of conditions present in the real world of men and things and their interplay.

The law of gravitation is a familiar example. By the force of gravity every object must seek the center of the earth. But does it? Atmospheric pressures with changing winds and weather blow not only feathers and kites but sometimes human bodies off the ground and through the air. Intricate man-made structures like airplanes and ocean liners, even Sputniks launched into outer space, manage, at least temporarily, to avoid seeking the center of the earth. The law of gravitation is not thereby defied or denied. In making things that float or fly or encircle the earth, gravitation must certainly be reckoned with; yet in the total complex of interacting circumstances many other forces and factors affect the product and its operation.

Still another matter is of overwhelming importance. The more we find personal wills impinging upon natural events, the less precisely can the course of these events be predicted or charted. The "personal equation" must never be overlooked. In spite of the determinist's attempt to make psychology into a purely natural science and hence to bring all human causation under the categories of natural law, the facts of experience stand in the way. In modern culture there is a curiously illogical combination of determinism and voluntarism in the assumption that all human choices are determined by natural circumstances and social conditioning; yet man is free to make unlimited improvements in his own status and that of his society.[9] Nevertheless, all the way from major world events, like the destinies of nations in a world war, to the most commonplace and ordinary, such as turning on the ignition of an automobile and releasing the brake, human wills make a difference in natural events. It is apparent that as man in important aspects of his life is limited by nature, so do personal wills affect enormously what happens in nature.

3. Miracle and law

The bearing of the meaning and limitations of natural law upon miracle is important from several angles. In the first place the things that happen within the natural order, even though they occur within structures of regularity that may be described by laws, are still miracles if they call forth wonder, surprise, and a sense of gratitude to God. Augustine, though he knew nothing of natural law in the modern meaning of the term, expressed this sense of the miraculous throughout God's world as aptly as it has ever been put. In *The City of God* he wrote:

Is not the universe itself a miracle, yet visible and of God's making? Nay, all the miracles done in this world are less than the world itself, the heaven and earth and all therein; yet God made them all, and after a manner that man cannot conceive or comprehend. For though these visible miracles of nature be now no more admired, yet ponder them wisely, and they are more astonishing than the strangest: for man is a greater miracle than all that he can work.[10]

A second aspect of the relation of miracle to law lies in the

[9] See Reinhold Niebuhr, *Faith and History*, pp. 79 ff., for a searching analysis of the consequences of this confusion.
[10] *Op. cit.*, Bk. X, xii.

fact that natural laws are abstractions, not descriptions of concrete circumstances that in actuality "come mixed." Miracles occur within a combination of many interrelated forces. For example, in the case of a healing deemed miraculous, who can say how much is to be attributed to the body's natural recuperative powers, how much to medical care if this has been given, how much to faithful and competent nursing, how much to the individual's composure of mind and will to live, how much to his total Christian faith, and how much to prayer by himself or another? The empirical fact is that a person seriously ill recovers when the doctors had given him up. It is equally an empirical fact that with so many factors involved, it is impossible to say which one, if any single one, is determinative. Rather, we do well to thank God without presuming to more knowledge than we have! What we can know about natural causes we should know; yet in most events deemed miraculous there is no exact tracing of causal sequences even by the wisest mind.

A third aspect of the matter is perhaps the most crucial, for it centers in God's relation to the total process. We have said repeatedly that God does not have to come in from without to effect changes in nature. There is no need for Him, in the colloquial but striking words of De Lawd in "Green Pastures," to "rare back and pass a miracle." To quote Augustine again, "We say that all portents are contrary to nature; but they are not so. For how is that contrary to nature which happens by the will of God, since the will of so mighty a Creator is certainly the nature of each created thing?" [11] God is present, as sustaining power, in all nature. Yet God is more than power; He is personal love. He is working out His long and loving purpose within both human and natural events. There is no reason to suppose that He must work out these purposes within a single pattern.

We noted that those events are most often called miraculous in which, out of a deep and critical need, God's saving help is seen to be so unmistakably present as to call forth wonder and

[11] *Ibid.*, Bk. XXI, viii.

the response of grateful faith. This is true whether it is the miracle of spiritual rebirth or some physical escape from death or danger. In either event the responsive Christian feels that he has indubitable evidence of God's personal, loving concern. Whether this happens within the known laws of nature or at variance with them is inconsequential compared with the all-important fact that God has acted in power and in love, and life is different.

There is no barrier in Christian faith to the belief that God works out His purposes for individual human lives and for the world by the use of "His own law-abiding powers." And the evidence of experience supports this view. As certainly as we know that men do not gather grapes from thorns or figs from thistles, we know that God does not work in a random or haphazard manner. Yet neither does God work out His purposes mechanically. There is an almost limitless variety in the way in which even human persons impinge on each other's lives. There are great regularities, but there are also great differences. God is Personal Spirit, and spirit whether in God or man uses nature as the medium and instrument of purpose. There is no single, one-track way.

At this point an important distinction and at the same time an important bond of connection must again be stressed. All that occurs in nature occurs by the power of God. There is no independent efficacy in nature to thwart God and prove Him the powerless puppet of natural forces, nor does some malevolent power manipulate it. As surely as nature's laws are God's law, whatever happens in nature happens by the power of God. It is an all-important expression of the constancy of God's purpose that our world is put together with regularities of nature which in large measure can be predicted and utilized for our security and happiness. Yet God's constancy of purpose does not mean that every specific event, however destructive of human good, is the specific expression of a divine purpose. As we saw in Chapter Four, God's maintenance of His orderly universe means that He sometimes permits what He does not will. There are natural

157

calamities and premature, violent deaths over which God must grieve, as do you and I, and where possible He calls on us to prevent them.

Within limits but over wide areas of existence we can prevent them. In conquering disease germs, harnessing flood waters, and irrigating arid lands, man uses nature's laws for human good. The laws are not set aside; they are understood and utilized. "Law is not a means of imprisonment to personality, but of release." [12] It is legitimate to believe that God also serves human good without violation of His laws, though within limits set not by His power but by His infinite wisdom. Again we must affirm that when man so obviously can use nature's regularities to achieve his ends within a system where there is both fixity and flexibility, we cannot suppose that God does less.

So there is a place within God's world both for the regularities of nature and for miracles that stir in us a sense of wonder at God's works. By both our lives are blessed; in both we see God's providence. But let us turn now to a very important consideration for Christian faith—the miracles of the Bible.

4. Miracles in the Bible

It would be folly to suggest the possibility of "explaining" all the biblical miracles. Miracle, we have said, by its very nature suggests wonder and amazement. Were it possible to give a natural explanation of everything recorded in the Bible, almost inevitably the sense of wonder would fade away. Miracle is based not simply on our ignorance but on the *mysterium tremendum* that is the will and work of God.

Yet, on the other hand, miracle, whether in the Bible or in modern life, needs to be understood, as far as we can understand it, within a frame of reference that is more than simple, blank mystery. In that literary classic, *Through the Looking-glass,* the White Queen tells Alice that she "can believe six impossible things before breakfast." The Bible is not a realm of fantasy in

[12] Fosdick, op. cit., p. 160.

which any sort of impossible thing may happen and must be believed. It is the record of the most important thing in all the world—God's dealings in judgment, love, and mercy with His people. This is certainly worthy of the best understanding we can bring to it!

As a framework for interpreting the miracles of the Bible, at least four basic tenets are necessary. The first of these we have already referred to in summarizing the stages through which the meaning of miracle has passed. The biblical writers were sure that whatever happens in nature, God does. Man might sin against the holy will of God, thus bringing divine judgment and disaster on his nation and himself; yet God remains Lord of all that He has made. This is stated with marvelous beauty and power in the later chapters of the Book of Job and in the nature poetry of the Psalms, but it is implied throughout the Bible. And this, we have seen, is basic to our own understanding of God's wonderful works. Untroubled by ideas of scientific regularity and precision, the biblical writers were not tempted to devise ideas of a deistic divine intervention. Yet as certainly as we must affirm God's activity in all nature, they saw the immanent presence of the transcendent God throughout His world.

And, in the second place, they saw that God is not limited to doing things always in exactly the same manner. They knew as well as we know that iron usually sinks, but if God chose to make an axe head swim, they saw no reason to doubt the event. So, too, if it were not an axe head but the physical body of Jesus walking on the surface of the water, the story did not arouse incredulity.

We must proceed with caution at this point, for in their assumption of the power of God to vary His usual ways of working, the biblical writers undoubtedly were right. With God all things are possible! Yet from the standpoint of the regularity with which we see God working in nature—a standpoint which the biblical writers in a prescientific age could not have—there is reason to doubt that as many deviations from the usual order occurred as are recorded in the Bible. It is not the possibility but

159

the probability of the literal accuracy of many of the miracle stories that is in question.

This brings us to a third basic tenet, which is the need to understand the Bible in its total historical setting. No full understanding is possible which does not take into account the intervals of time within which the miracle stories were passed on in the oral tradition before being written down, presumably gathering accretions as they were told; the tendency not only in the Hebrew-Christian tradition but almost universally for such stories to cluster about the names of great personages; the natural tendency of a prescientific age to believe without question anything adding luster or meaning to a person or event.

It is virtually a commonplace of biblical interpretation that the more nearly contemporary the writing, the less it contains of puzzling deviations from what is today recognized as God's usual and orderly ways of working. For example the Old Testament stories of David and his successors, beginning with II Samuel and running through I and II Kings, are based primarily, though not wholly, upon contemporary court records and are remarkably vivid, unmiraculous accounts of an important epoch in Israel's history. The writings of the prophets, being firsthand or nearly firsthand messages,[13] contain far less in the way of miracle, save for the all-encompassing miracle of God's grace, than do the orally told and retold stories of the Pentateuch. So also in the New Testament Paul's letters, the earliest writing, reflect much less in the way of specific miracle stories than do the Gospels, though everywhere the marvel of God's "unspeakable gift" in Christ shines through.

The fourth tenet is of great importance. Every miracle story in the Bible *means something*. Let me hasten to say that it is

[13] It is doubtful that any book in the Old Testament has come to us without some change from its original form. Yet in comparison with the J, E, D, and P narratives the writings of the prophets have undergone relatively little alteration. Likewise, the court records above referred to underwent editorial changes but are more authentic than the postexilic accounts of the same period found in I and II Chronicles.

160

not necessary or desirable to try to draw a hidden allegorical meaning out of everything in the Bible! To do this, as for example, to suppose that the three messengers from the Lord who appeared before Abraham's tent to announce the birth of a son to Sarah in her old age foreshadows the three persons of the Trinity, is to distort the Bible, not to interpret it. Yet every miracle story in the Bible, including this one, meant something to the person or persons who believed, told, and wrote it. Always it meant the power of God, but often also, as in God's covenant with Abraham and His promise to make him the father of a mighty nation, it meant the goodness and the guiding, providential hand of God. Had not the story meant something—and often something great—it would have been forgotten before ever being recorded.

A miracle story as it is recorded in the Bible bears somewhat the same relation to factual history as a portrait bears to a photograph. The camera catches every line just as it is; a portrait has indeed a basis in reality, but it is an interpretative portrayal. The story takes some such event as Jesus' calming the fears of the disciples in a storm at sea, disregards—as the first century could more easily than we—any scientific questions about the law of gravitation, and portrays our Lord as walking on the water. The meaning of the story then and its meaning now is found in the words, "Take heart, it is I; have no fear." A similar story is recorded in all three of the Synoptic Gospels,[14] but with the miraculous element in the calming of the waves when the terrified disciples awoke their Lord who was asleep in the stern of the boat. What exactly happened? We do not know. This may have been two events or one. Something certainly happened, but the account of it may have undergone some change in the telling before the Gospel narratives were written. What it meant then and what it means now is found in our Lord's answer to the question, "Why are you afraid? Have you no faith?" (Mark

[14] Matt. 8:23-27; Mark 4:35-41; Luke 8:22-25.

4:40.) *That* answer is constant from age to age, and in it lies the heart of the meaning of providence.

So integral are the miracle stories to the gospel narratives that we cannot disregard or eliminate them. They are indubitably there in great profusion, even to the raising of the dead. It is not so indubitable what we shall think either about their historical accuracy or their meaning, but of the two the meaning is both the clearer and the more important.

About any miracle story three questions may be asked. *Could it happen?* Yes, if we do not doubt the power of God to work in ways other than His usual courses. In particular the Son of God may well be thought to have possessed unusual powers, and there is a fitness about the miracles of Jesus that makes us hesitate to say they could not have happened. The supreme miracle of the Bible, and indeed of all Christian faith, lies in the incarnation, the self-giving even to the cross, the resurrection, and the living presence of Jesus Christ as our Lord. To lives touched and illumined by this overwhelming miracle, it does not seem inappropriate to believe that Jesus had a power to work miracles that ordinary men do not have. Always, we must recall, he refused to do "signs and wonders" simply to attract attention or show off his powers; he often asked not to have what he had done told lest it be misunderstood. When he performed miracles it was always in love, compassion, and helpfulness to people, and for this purpose it is not unreasonable to suppose that the Creator of all nature gave him unusual powers over nature. The testimony of Peter to the early Christian community may well be ours today. "You know . . . how God anointed Jesus of Nazareth with the Holy Spirit and with power; how he went about doing good and healing all that were oppressed by the devil, for God was with him." (Acts 10:36-38.)

These miracles of Jesus are, of course, not the only ones in the Bible. Miracles appear many times in the Old Testament and to a less frequent but still significant degree in the accounts of the early days of the Church. Could they have happened? Yes, if God had a sufficient reason within His purposes for their occurrence. Only the reign of an inflexible, self-sufficient, natural order closes the door to the possibility. We must repeat, the Creator of all nature is not required to work always in just one way.

A second question, however, may affect our judgment. *Did it happen?* Here what is involved is not the possibility of the miracle's having occurred but the historical accuracy of the account. All the principles of biblical interpretation that have been noted are at this point relevant. There is no irreverence in supposing that even among the miracles attributed to Jesus some, such as the cursing of the barren fig tree, were originally parables that in the reporting got changed to miracles. Our decision as to the actual historicity of a story will need to be based on as careful a study as can be made of authorship, date, literary form, and contemporary setting—a study for which trained biblical scholarship is needed, though fortunately the results of such study are now widely available. Our decision will also rest in part on a sense of fitness, on which not all can be expected to agree. To suppose, for example, that in the story of Elisha God caused two she-bears to come out of the woods to mutilate forty-two boys who mocked at his bald head seems to me less credible, because less worthy of God, than the restoration of the Shunammite's son or the cure of Naaman's leprosy.[15]

Since at some points we do not know exactly what happened, we had better acknowledge that we do not. Yet this need not plunge us into skepticism or, as the literalists are wont to claim, lead us to throw out all that is in the Bible. There is much of which we can be sure, centering in the supreme miracle of God's gift to mankind in Jesus Christ our Lord. And when we examine what is recorded as to the deeds of Jesus, there too we find an adequate basis for believing that in its central features the record gives a true report.

In the Gospel narratives no Christian can doubt that "mighty works" took place in the healing of men's souls. Though we do

[15] II Kings 2:23-25; 4:32-37; 5:1-14.

not, like the people of the first century, speak of the restoration of disordered minds to sanity as the driving out of demons, Christ still brings peace and strength to disordered spirits. That he changed the currents of men's lives in an amazing way as he forgave their sins and called them to discipleship can hardly be questioned. Such miracles have been happening ever since by the power of God in Christ and are happening today.

Furthermore, there is a high degree of certainty that Jesus wrought miracles of physical as well as spiritual healing. It fits consistently with all we know of him to suppose that he cared about the bodies as well as the souls of men and used his God-given powers in helpfulness. As was indicated in the preceding chapter, healing through faith does not now seem so medically preposterous as it once did. God still heals bodies as well as souls in ways that seem miraculous—in hospitals, at Roman Catholic shrines, in Protestant churches, and counseling rooms and homes.

It is when we come to the so-called nature miracles, such as walking on the sea, changing water into wine, miraculously multiplying the loaves and fishes, or restoring to bodily life those already dead, that more serious questions of historicity arise. It is at this point that those minds demanding a scientific explanation of everything are most likely to balk, while those to whom the natural order is inconsequential see no problem. The wiser course lies between. We cannot dismiss these stories simply as folk tales devised to prove Jesus' superiority as a wonderworker, as even some eminent New Testament scholars tend to do,[16]

---

[16] Both Rudolf Bultmann and Martin Dibelius regard the miracle stories of the Gospels as possessing such a remarkable similarity to Jewish and Hellenistic miracle narratives that their source is a recasting of these tales to prove Jesus' superiority over all other gods and saviors. "Jewish-Christian narrators would make Jesus the hero of well-known legends of prophets or rabbis. Gentile-Christian narrators would hand on stories of gods, saviours and miracle-workers, re-cast as applying to the Christian Saviour." (M. Dibelius, From Tradition to Gospel [London: Nicholson and Watson, 1934], p. 100.) Without denying that the stories were told and retold to prove the superiority of Jesus as Saviour, it is still not necessary to depreciate their historicity to this extent. Alan Richardson in The Miracle-Stories of the Gospels, pp. 22-28, takes sharp issue with the Bultmann-Dibelius theory.

nor need we feel obligated to accept them as fully accurate history. Something happened—we do not know exactly what— that left an indelible impression on those who knew of the occurrence. We may form theories as to what did happen, always leaving open the possibility that our theory may be wrong. What we may *not* do is to miss the message of God's providential care that was so vividly present in the thought of those who told these stories in the first century and ought equally to be present in our thought today.

This brings us to the third question to be asked. *What does it mean?* This, we have already noted, is the most crucial question of all. To the New Testament writers and indeed, to the biblical writers as a whole, every story that was remembered and told meant something. The inconsequential does not arrest attention and is soon buried in the forgotten past. Even an apparently trivial incident, like an unusual catch of fish or the finding of a shekel in a fish's mouth, was taken to mean the presence and power and goodness of God.

Do we need the miracle stories in order to believe that "God was in Christ?"—in one sense yes and in another no. In the early Church the marvelous accounts of the deeds of Jesus soon took on a special meaning as a demonstration that He was the long-expected Messiah and the Christ, the Son of the living God. Along with the stories of His birth and of His death and resurrection they were told and retold in witness to the mighty acts of God and His saving power through Christ. If we adhere to the meaning of miracle as God's wonderful works, evoking awe and reverence, gratitude and praise, then we can find no higher miracle than what Jesus was and did. Yet His divinity does not hinge upon the miracles; rather, His divinity makes the miracles appropriate. It is what Jesus *did* and *does* in human lives in compassionate love that attests Him as our Lord and Savior.

We noted Augustine's saying that man is a greater miracle than any of his works. This is true, and it is well to remember this is in a day when scientific achievement fills men's minds,

165

giving "creature comforts" and satisfactions at many points but also filling the soul with deep apprehension at a possible third world war and the destruction of mankind. Man *is* a miracle, for he is the high point of God's wonderful creation. Yet the greatest miracle of all is Jesus Christ, the God-man, bearer of God's power and love and forgiving, saving mercy. So great is this miracle that before the wonder of Jesus all others seem inconsequential.

We conclude, therefore, that miracles are real, though not in the deistic structure of thought in which they are commonly conceived, that they *did* occur in Bible times, that they *have* *occurred* throughout the history of Christian thought and life, and that they occur *now*. Surpassing all other miracles, whether we find them in the wonder and glory of God's world or what happens in individual lives to reveal God's providential care, the greatest miracle is Jesus Christ. The supreme miracle that can happen in any life is to feel His healing touch in the spiritual sickness that sin has plunged us into, and in pain of body or distress of soul to find renewal and rebirth through Him.

Yet ever in the offing death confronts us. Is the miracle of such renewal and rebirth for this life only or for eternity? Our Christian faith promises the latter. It affirms that through God's miracle of grace Christ is the hope of the world, now and forever. Accordingly, in the concluding chapter we must look at the relations of time to eternity in God's providence and at the Christian's hope of eternal life.

Chapter Eight

OF TIME AND ETERNITY

THIS STUDY CANNOT PROPERLY BE CONCLUDED WITHOUT FURTHER
consideration of that basic structure of existence within which
God's providence is both manifest and promised, namely, time
and eternity. Some references, indeed, we have been obliged to
make all along the way, for the God who creates and redeems
in time guides and sustains us providentially within the earthly,
historical scene and offers the hope of eternal life to those who
love and serve Him. We have not attempted to probe the whole
mystery of how He does this, for much is hidden from our earth-
bound eyes, but only to discover and state as consistently as possible the grounds of our faith. It is appropriate that we now try
to indicate something of the Christian faith in what lies beyond
history, as far as we can see it, in relation to what lies within it.

1. What is time?

Time impinges upon us all, and within its sway our lives are
set. Save for the years of infancy and senility, there are few who
do not have to give close attention to the clock and the calendar. Ours is a particularly time-conscious era, and one of the
most difficult problems of human adjustment is to meet the
demands of time's inexorable ongoing. This is true both in the
details and the totality of our existence. Too much hurry means
worry lest we fail to "make it," speeding on highways, frantic
overexertion beyond the body's normal capacity, high blood
pressure, and heart attacks. Not a few of the world's most useful
persons, including Christian leaders, have died from the pressure
of meeting appointments in a too crowded schedule. On the

other hand too little sense of time spells indolence and ineffi-
ciency—to say nothing of the irritation and inconvenience of
those who must wait for the laggards! Relatively few persons in
our overstimulated, hurrying generation appear to have acquired
the fine art of getting one's responsibilities met without haste
or waste and then of relaxing comfortably in the leisure that
ensues.

In part this tyranny of time is a phenomenon of contemporary
Western culture, as the American in the Orient soon discovers.
There time is taken much less seriously, and one must expect to
wait for things to get done. Yet no man anywhere can escape its
irrevocable advance, bringing with it for awhile growth and
opportunity but beyond these disintegration, decay and death.

> Time, like an ever-rolling stream,
> Bears all its sons away;
> They fly forgotten, as a dream
> Dies at the opening day.[1]

Or do they? That is the question which makes the relation of
time to eternity of consummate importance in every religion.

That time, even apart from eternity, is important seems clear
enough. But what *is* time? This is by no means self-evident, and
diverse philosophies of history center about varying interpretations of it. "As Augustine once remarked, when nobody asks us
what time is, we know; but when we try to explain it, we do not
know." [2] The fact is that we are a great deal better at saying "what
time it is" than "what time is!" Nevertheless, both philosophers
and theologians for many centuries have been making the attempt. Whether as a naturalistic "process" philosophy, a humanistic doctrine of inevitable progress, existentialism in its various
forms, or a Christian philosophy of history, the meaning of time
occupies much attention in contemporary thought.

---

[1] Isaac Watts, stanza five of "O God, Help in Ages Past."
[2] Roger Hazelton, *op. cit.*, p. 87.

This is not the place to canvass these various views. They are complex, and their implications would carry us far beyond our present concern.[3] I shall attempt, however, to give some hints as to the meaning of time as this bears on the view of providence presented in the preceding chapters, and in particular, on the relations of time to eternal life.

There are three kinds of time, all related aspects of one total structure, but impinging upon us with different meanings. All are related to God's providential care and leading, though not in the same way or with the same degree of intensity.

The first of these I shall call objective time, though its more usual designation, when an adjective is deemed necessary, is chronological or calendar time. It is the kind of time science uses in its measurements, though for its larger astronomical computations science goes beyond the calendar to light years, and modern physics, substituting a plurality of "pointer-readings," questions the complete objectivity of time. For ordinary purposes, however, objective time is the kind wherein one hundred years makes a century, 365 days make a year, save for one year in four when an extra day is added to catch up with the sun, twenty-four hours make a day, sixty minutes make an hour, sixty seconds make a minute—all of this in total disregard of what we do in this time or whether we exist at all. It is God-given in the sense that it is based upon the earth's rotation on its axis and revolutions about the sun; it is man-made in that the main features of our calendar were set up by the Babylonians, revised under Julius Caesar, and corrected again in the sixteenth century to constitute the presently used Gregorian calendar.

This objective time, at first glance, does not seem to have anything to do with providence. It is simply something given—a fixed frame of reference about which we can do nothing. Yet like the other fixities of nature considered in previous chapters,

---

[3] See Reinhold Niebuhr's *Faith and History,* and in particular Chapter III, "Time as the Stage of History," for a penetrating analysis of classical and modern views. The present writer does not accept all of Niebuhr's conclusions but finds his presentation, as always, trenchant and suggestive.

the objectivity of time is a great boon, an incomparably great blessing bestowed by the all-wise Creator. Without it there could be no framework for achievement, no planning ahead, no assessing of the past. Without it there could be no common life, and life, if it existed at all, would have no sort of ordered continuity. In short apart from the objectivity of time there could be no history. Human history does not require the particular calendar we have. There was history before men began to date events from the birth of Christ and again before the Gregorian supplanted the Julian calendar. Yet history occurs only in a time setting that is objective to everybody within it. It is a large part of the general providence of God that He has given us this objective framework of time in which to work out with Him our individual destiny and that of the human race.

A second kind of time may be called experienced time. This is the mind's awareness of change in the passage of time and the occurrence of events. In a dreamless sleep or some other form of unconsciousness there is no such awareness and time seems nonexistent. In waking consciousness, however, some moments seem interminably long while again the months and days fly by with incredible rapidity. The minutes while one awaits news from the operating room where a loved one hovers between life and death can seem an eternity. One looks forward for months with great eagerness to a vacation trip, a reunion with loved ones, or some other high experience; it is "over in no time" when it comes. Since this book may be read by some ministers, it may be à propos to quote the remark of a homiletics professor who says that in reality there is no such thing as a long or a short sermon, only those sermons that seem long or that seem short!

This kind of time does not cancel out the reality of objective time. We have had to use the verb "seem" in the previous paragraph because of an implicit recognition that clock and calendar time is independent of our awareness. Yet this experienced time is a very large part of what personality is made of. It involves not only an awareness of change in the passage of time but of meaning in events. It is here that our loves and aspirations, our

170

sense of achievement, and our yearning for new and different experiences are located.

The honored Quaker scholar and saint, Rufus M. Jones, used to refer somewhat whimsically to the life story of the oldest man in the Bible, "Thus all the days of Methuselah were nine hundred and sixty-nine years; and he died" (Gen. 5:27). Methuselah begot some sons and daughters in this period, no mean achievement, but what else? His fame rests only on duration, not on quality of living. It is the experience that is packed into one's chronological years, not their bare extension, that matters most. Judged by this standard, Rufus Jones himself, with his eighty-five years of rich usefulness to God and man, lived a life that for fullness is seldom equaled.

It is apparent that what we have called experienced time is not wholly a private matter. It is subjective in the sense that what is experienced varies from person to person, and the same event may seem long or short to different persons, even as it may seem good or bad. However, its effects spill over into the public domain both as an index of the kind of person one is and as a contribution or detriment to the lives of others. It lacks the inflexibility of calendar time, but it has a very effective potency of its own.

It is at this point that providence becomes relevant. We have admitted frankly that the same event may be viewed as coincidence or providence according to one's presuppositions and point of view. There is no way of proving to the skeptic beyond the shadow of a doubt that the hand of God determined the outcome of an event. This is because experienced time is always *interpreted* time. No event that relates to human life is ever viewed with bare, completely unbiased detachment. The meaning taken to it always determines in some measure the meaning taken from it. Yet to one who grants the reality of God's providential care, the faith that the times are in His hand [4] gives both personal peace and social dynamic. Experienced time then be-

---

[4] Cf. Ps. 31:14, 15.

comes God's time, not in the sense that all events are as He would have them, but that He is the Lord of history "in whose will is our peace."

A third kind of time, emerging within both objective and experienced time but with a special meaning, is *kairos*. In contrast with *chronos* or chronological time, *kairos* means the time of opportunity and demand.[5] It is strategic time, the *now* of decision, when what is decided and done will affect the currents of the future. Though it is nowhere in the Bible analyzed as a special aspect of time, it is deeply imbedded in the biblical point of view, giving a sense of urgency to the need to obey and serve God. It is stated with great clarity in Moses' address to the people of Israel:

I call heaven and earth to witness against you this day, that I have set before you life and death, blessing and curse; therefore choose life, that you and your descendants may live, loving the Lord your God, obeying his voice, and cleaving to him; for that means life to you and length of days. (*Deut. 30:19-20.*)

This note is reiterated again and again in the messages of the prophets. In the New Testament it appears in the oft-repeated, "Repent, for the kingdom of heaven is at hand." The same sense of urgency breathes through all of Paul's writing and comes to overt expression in, "Behold, now is the acceptable time; behold, now is the day of salvation" (II Cor. 6:2).

This is the biblical way of saying, "We live in a time of crisis." Whether a national crisis, as in much of Old Testament history, or a personal crisis it means opportunity, demand, decision. It is the Bible's primary message that only in decision for God and acceptance of His grace at the cost of faithful obedience to His will is our salvation. And this cannot be put off indefinitely; *now* is the time.

This sense of urgency in national affairs has become a domi-

[5] See Paul Tillich, *The Interpretation of History*, Part II, Chap. 2, for a much fuller statement of the meaning and significance of *kairos*.

nant note within the vicissitudes of the cold war, and "too little and too late" has become a common expression both of pathos and of condemnatory judgment. So also in personal life, both the theology of crisis[6] and much of current evangelism stress the peril of the soul if one does not decide immediately for Christ. There is significance in these warnings and demands for action, whether national or personal, though there is always danger that a valid warning and demand for decision may turn into an alarmist mood. Not hysteria but hope should be the accompaniment and result of a sense of *kairos*.

Kairos is intimately connected with providence, for in the biblical sense it is not simply the state of society that challenges complacency, but it is God who speaks to say, "Therefore choose life!" Both in the covenant relation with Israel and in the New Israel of the Church, it is God who presents the opportunity, makes the demand, calls for the decision. His providence is open, but His protection and salvation are conditional; there must be acceptance and response.

Not only does *kairos* in this sense place the initiative both in judgment and redemption with God, but it assumes the possibility and the necessity of free human decision. If providence were predestination, there would be no such thing as *kairos*; there would be only the destiny within time and eternity that God ordains. But since providence never cancels human freedom, we do stand always at the point of decision, and sometimes at points of greater opportunity and urgency than others.

To summarize this section, there is objective, chronological time within which everything we do and all the events of history take place—the gift of God and a primary blessing, though we too often let it become a tyrannical master. There is the time we experience, and into it we put such meaning as our varied personalities determine. Within it God stands ready always to guard and guide us, though we may fail to acknowledge His presence.

---

[6] A term sometimes used as a synonym for the new orthodoxy, stressing not the social but the personal crisis of man as he stands under the judgment of God. See Emil Brunner, *The Theology of Crisis*.

And there is the time of critical opportunity and demand, wherein God speaks both through outer circumstances and in the inner life to say, "You must choose." These are not three kinds of time in dissociation from each other; rather, they stand in concentric circles. God is in them all, and His providence is in them all; yet He comes to us in different ways. Neither time nor His action can be reduced to one flat, barren structure.

2. What is eternity?

What is eternity? The very putting of this question suggests presumption. Time we know something about. We live in it and have to watch it constantly. But who knows anything about eternity? We have no empirical evidence of it, and the dead, who by faith may be assumed to live in it, do not come back to tell us.[7]

Yet we must have some idea of eternity. Not only is it basic to biblical faith, but the word appears very commonly in ordinary speech. Whether as the title of a best seller, *From Here to Eternity*, or as a reference to what the careless automobile driver will be plunged into if he takes foolhardy chances, we talk about it frequently. In a more serious mood, when death takes away a loved one, to contemplate it is virtually inevitable.

Eternity, like time, has three distinguishable but somewhat related meanings. Yet unlike time only one of these is adequate for Christian thought and a satisfactory basis for the hope of eternal life. We shall look at the first two for such suggestiveness as they present, but in the main to reject them.

One meaning of eternity is endless duration. It is temporality, though usually without explicit reference to the calendar, stretched on beyond individual earthly life and beyond any human life on the planet. Sometimes, though not always, such temporality is also thought of as indefinitely antecedent to crea-

---

[7] This is not to deny the possibility of spirit communication. Some very intelligent minds have believed in it. I have not seen evidence enough to convince me of it but am willing to leave the door open to the possibility. The point here is that such spirit communications as have been reported by those who believe in it give no assured knowledge of the nature of eternity.

tion, so that an eternal creation is taken to mean that time never had a beginning. The ordinary Christian view is that time began when creation took place, though there are logical difficulties in this position which led Augustine, as he wrestled with the problem, to assert that "we can reasonably say there was another time when this time was not; but not the merest simpleton could say there was a time when there was no time." [8]

As indicated in Chapter Three, I believe we should be exceedingly cautious about affirming how or when time began. It is shrouded in the mystery of creation. It is consistent with Christian faith either to believe that God has been eternally creating His world, and hence from God's perspective time had no beginning, or to believe that with the creation of the world God created time also. All that is essential is to affirm God as the Creator and the ultimate dependence of the world upon His will and creativity. This which is essential is assured both by Christian faith and by logical consistency with a theistic interpretation of the universe.

But our problem at this point is not with eternity in its past but in its future, if we take it to mean endless duration. What, if anything, can we say about it?

When eternity is conceived as endless future time, it is usually set in contrast to time within earthly history. It is then conceived to refer either to what lies beyond the death of the individual or beyond all human existence on earth. These two issues, though related, are not identical. Contemporary theological writing deals much more with the second than with the first, as is illustrated by the fact that in the long and profound discussion of the theme, "Christ, the hope of the world," which preceded the Evanston Assembly of the World Council of Churches, attention was given almost exclusively to eschatology in its corporate significance. However, since providence is related most intimately to the destiny of the individual, we must look mainly at eternity from this point of view.

[8] Augustine, *op. cit.*, Bk. XII, 15.

It is certain that eternity, as endless existence beyond death, cannot be conceived in clock or calendar time. Aside from the fact that beyond earthly existence we can hardly conceive of a physical sun or rotating earth as the measure of time, it affronts one's sense of fitness to suppose that "all the saints who from their labors rest" are getting older and older in calendar years. They would be far beyond the recorded age of Methuselah in the case of those who died in the early days of the Christian era! Though there is a certain appropriateness in the anticipation of fellowship with the great souls of the past, as Socrates suggested in his meditations preceding death,[9] the imagination balks at the thought of introducing earth-bound measurements into what lies beyond earthly existence. It is, indeed, the difficulty of introducing, and on the other hand, of eliminating a space-time setting that makes the entire concept to eternal life seem to many minds nebulous to the point of absurdity.

Yet deeper than the difficulty presented to the imagination is the barrenness of endless duration, if this is the only or the chief characteristic of eternal life. For belief in eternal life to be maintained, it need not appeal to egoistic self-interest, or the will to perpetuation of prestige or power, or any other form of wishful thinking. Yet if belief in eternal life is to have any vitality, it must find rootage in the deeper intuitions of feeling and faith. And it is doubtful that any thoughtful person would greatly desire eternal life or find challenge in its hope, if it meant only a bare and endless duration. Though in moments of overstrenuous activity one may look to Heaven as a place of rest, who would want simply to live on and on and on and on and on and on ad infinitum? It is a quality of life in God's nearer presence and in fellowship with loved ones, not mere extension of time, that makes eternal life a perennial Christian hope.

Accordingly, we must reject endless duration as our definition of eternity. Yet we do not need to eliminate from our thought of it the central note of what was called in the previous section

[9] Plato, Phaedo, 63, 69.

176

experienced time. Its framework, indeed, must be other than that provided by the sun and the calendar, but God can give us such a setting as we need for personal experience. And within such experience we may well believe that there is continuity. Neither endless duration nor static fixity but a continuity of experience within which there is a place for change, activity, and even growth is consistent with the Christian hope of eternal life.

A second meaning of eternity is timelessness. In sharp contrast with the injection of duration into eternity this is the denial of all temporal relevance and character to eternity. It is the equivalent of changelessness and implies a kind of static fixity against which the perpetual "becoming" and flux of existence are to be measured.

This view of eternity has had a long history, appearing among the Greeks in Parmenides and the Eleatic emphasis on Being as contrasted with the Heraclitic philosophy of Becoming. It appears in Plato's thought in his eternal archetypes, or forms, of which all concrete things are but the copy, though scholars differ as to whether Plato held to an absolute disjunction between time and eternity in view of his famous statement that "time is the moving image of eternity." [10] It survives in modern thought in the recognition that mathematical and logical relations, like the multiplication table or the rules of the syllogism in formal logic, have a timelessness and fixity not to be attributed to any concrete thing.

But it is the religious meaning of eternity in this sense that must concern us. Since God is the ground of all being, changeless in love, wisdom, and power in the midst of the changing flux of historical existence, it is appropriate to speak of God as the Eternal. From this it is but a short step to identify eternity with God. In fact it is common—though I believe confusing—

[10] Hazelton, op. cit., pp. 119-22, gives a persuasive defense of the view that Plato meant by this to indicate not only a contrast but a profound connection between time and eternity, an "inclusive transcendence" of time in eternity that comes closer to Christianity than does any other non-Christian view.

usage to speak of the historical and the eternal as if one meant simply the human and the divine.

We are on safe ground to assert that all that is eternal is derived from God. If God is Ultimate Being, such questionable permanence as nature possesses and such eternity as may be hoped for in human existence are from God's hand. But does this equate eternity with timelessness or a static transcendence of nature and history? By no means.

So to conceive eternity is very unsatisfactory with regard to both God and man. God is indeed the Eternal. Yet in the biblical and Christian view of God as personal Creator, Judge, Redeemer, and Father He cannot be thought of as indifferent to time. In sharp contrast with the characteristic Greek view of history as recurrent world cycles, the Hebrew-Christian view centers in the conviction that God is the Lord of history and that history moves forward as a great drama of judgment and redemption through the activity of God within the human scene. Both the covenant with Israel and the new covenant through the Incarnation, the Cross, and the Resurrection of Jesus Christ presuppose this view. These "mighty acts" and all of God's other mighty acts are supremely meaningful because they bespeak, not a transcendent Eternal indifferent to time and history, but a transcendent-immanent God—or as the Bible puts it, a living God—who is ever above and beyond us but who is also forever with us and forever active.

If it is important to conceive of God's eternity as something other than timelessness, so is it with man's. This is not to imply that man's eternity must in all respects be like God's. Man's eternity is derivative, not ultimate; it is God's gift. Of this we can be sure, even though there is much we should like to know about it that is hidden from us. Some hold that only Christians receive this gift; others hold that the supremely loving God opens the door of eternal life to those who have not accepted Christ and seeks even beyond the grave to win them to Himself. This is a vital point, but one on which we must be content to let opinions differ.[11] The point which is crucial to the meaning of man's eternity is that it is God's gift of continued existence beyond bodily death in a realm neither of bare duration nor of static timelessness but of a greatly enhanced quality of life in God's nearer presence.

A third meaning of eternity, then, which I believe to be the true one, has its focus in the continuance of personal existence beyond the earthly scene. Personality, whether in God or man, transcends time but does not nullify the significance of time. Eternity in God means that His long purposes are above and beyond all history; yet He is ever active within the world of human events, guiding, guarding, sustaining His human children, conquering evil by redemptive love. This is just what providence means. It is stated perfectly in the familiar words:

> The eternal God is your dwelling place,
> and underneath are the everlasting arms.
> (Deut. 33:27)

Eternity in man means that we, the recipients of God's love and providential care, are safe with Him not only within the vicissitudes and flux of history but in whatever lies beyond our mortal lives. In short God's time transcends history and is not bounded by its margins.

If this understanding of eternity is right, it is of vital importance that "beyond history" and "beyond mortality" should not be assumed to mean "beyond existence." Furthermore, if eternal life means more than empty duration or a static timelessness, it means that what happens here has its consequences in eternal life. The concept of *kairos* becomes very relevant. De-

---

[11] The main stream of the Christian tradition has held that there can be no repentance after death. However, the Roman Catholic Church has felt the need of assuming an intermediate state in purgatory, and another tradition running from Origen to Ferré has held that God's love cannot stop short of ultimate universal salvation. The present writer believes that death does not close the door to God's love and proffered forgiveness but sees no ground for assurance that all will respond to it. Furthermore, as will be indicated presently, decision in this life is too crucial to justify indifference or postponement.

cision for or against Christ, and in consequence, the taking of steps toward the growth of personality in love or its degradation in self-interest, become all-important. Recoil as we may from the artificiality of luring men to Christian decision or moral probity by the hope of heaven or the fear of hell, it remains true that without the vista of eternity man loses not only his highest hope but his greatest challenge. The eternity of personal existence must be linked with decisions made in time and history, or the continuity is abruptly sundered. Man's destiny, interwoven of the structure of natural circumstance, free decision, and God's providential care is not for time only but for eternity.

3. Journey's end

In English diction the word "end" has two quite distinct, though not wholly unrelated, meanings. The end of any activity may be its termination (*finis* in Latin) or its purpose, objective or goal (*telos* in Greek.) From this it comes about that something may be finished without being completed. When we come to the end of anything, whether the day's work, a long term of employment, a party, a vacation, the reading or the writing of a book, we come to a stopping point and must turn attention and energy in other directions. Life is full of such endings, some greeted joyously, some most reluctantly according to the quality and feeling tone of the experienced time. Yet it seldom happens that all the *ends* sought in such activities are fulfilled before they come to an *end*.

Within the biological duration of man's life all endings are relative. Some are very decisive and mark epochs of existence, as in the amputation of a limb or the termination of a marriage; yet memory links the past with the present, and anticipation makes possible the formation of new ends and goals for the future. The continuity of personal existence may appear to be completely shattered by some unexpected, crushing blow; yet while life and consciousness go on, it never is. Time can heal as well as destroy, and even as one waits in deep bereavement for "grief's slow wisdom" to do its work, one's shattered world is again rebuilt.

Yet there comes to man's mortal existence an irrevocable end. The death of a loved one may be surmounted, the better if there is a firm assurance of eternal life, but no man can escape the inevitable fact of his own death. He may delay it or hasten it; he may be relatively indifferent or deeply concerned about it; he cannot avoid it.

Though the historical future is veiled, there is serious ground for expectation that what happens to the individual may eventually happen to the entire human race. While no morbid anticipation of this end or time-setting schedules are in order, the possibility merits serious concern. Hence, the relations of history as a whole to eschatology are important and rightly hold a place in contemporary theology as they did in biblical thought. The issues are far-reaching, but it is not the purpose of this book to probe them. The focus of all history, without which there could be no corporate existence either on earth or beyond history, is the individual person. It is here also, as we have seen, that both the primary problems and certainties of God's providence are centered. Accordingly, we must look now, with caution but not with trepidation, at what God has promised beyond death for the individual.

It is precisely at the point of this great transition that "end" and "ends" become most significantly related. Biological life terminates; Christian faith affirms that by God's grace and providential care this is not the end of personal existence. Seldom, if ever, are all the ends—the hopes, the desires, the worthful aspirations—of an individual's life completed before his death. It is the Christian faith that as God's ends are eternal, so by His gift are the ends and the destiny of those to whom He imparts eternal life.

How does He impart it? Here we stand at the ultimate mystery of His providence, to walk by faith and not by sight. Yet we are not left wholly in darkness. We know all that we need to know. What I believe we can assert with a high degree of assurance

181

about the nature of the future life has been suggested earlier but may here be restated.

Eternal life is personal existence in continuity with the present life, but transfigured. The "immortality of influence" sometimes proposed as a substitute for personal immortality is no immortality at all, even though from the context of human society it is possible to say as does the apocryphal Wisdom of Solomon, "For in the memory of virtue is immortality." [12] Human society has no guarantee of permanence, and it is the person himself, not what he leaves behind him on earth, that in this matter is our focus of concern. Nor does "absorption in the Infinite," or the fading out of personality in Nirvana, or any other kind of loss of personal identity through a mystical union with God meet the issue. One lives *with* God as a person, not *in* God in some non-personal, nebulous merging of finite and infinite Being, if eternal life is real.

Yet it is obvious that such continuity of personal existence cannot be conceived without conceiving of change as well as permanence. Clearly, we shall not take our earthly bodies with us! There is a long tradition, not yet wholly abandoned, that thinks of resurrection as the restoration of the earthly body in the form it possessed before death. This has been reinforced by centuries of repetition of the words, "I believe in the resurrection of the body," and its effects range from silence before the mystery to aversion to the cremation of a corpse. However, this is not the soundest biblical position. Full of mystery to our earth-bound minds though the matter must be, there is no more Christian or more credible view than that which Paul states in I Cor. 15:

There are celestial bodies and there are terrestrial bodies; but the glory of the celestial is one, and the glory of the terrestrial is another. . . . So is it with the resurrection of the dead. What is sown is perishable, what is raised is imperishable. It is sown in dishonor, it is raised in glory. It is sown in weakness, it is raised in power. It is

[12] *Op. cit.*, IV, 1.

sown a physical body, it is raised a spiritual body. If there is a physical body, there is also a spiritual body. (*I Cor. 15:40, 42-44.*)

Note also that the figure of speech which Paul uses here, of the seed which is sown but dies to issue in new life as "God gives it a body as he has chosen," is a crystal-clear analogy of the union of permanence and change by the wisdom, power, and providence of God.

There is considerable difference of opinion in current theology as to whether resurrection or immortality is the more appropriate term for designating personal existence beyond bodily death. I have chosen to use the more inclusive and less controversial "eternal life," though with proper safeguards against error, either of the other terms may be used. Those who advocate "resurrection" and decry "immortality" do so on the grounds that the former is more biblical, referring to the entire person and not to his spirit only, and that the term "immortality of the soul" is too easily identified with a Greek idea of a natural (that is, not God-given) permanence of man's reason in contrast with the perishable nature of man's body. Those who prefer to retain the term "personal immortality" desire to avoid a mistaken idea of the resurrection of the flesh and can point to the fact that Paul certainly uses the term immortality in the same great paean of faith in which he affirms the conquest of death and the resurrection to a spiritual body by the power of God.[13]

What is essential to affirm is both continuity and change in personal existence by the power of God, with that spiritual victory in the entrance into new life which robs death of its sting. With God to guide and sustain us through eternity as through earthly time, there need be neither the uncertainty of the meaningless nor terror of the unknown as one confronts what lies beyond the grave.

Though we cannot give any pictorial description of the future life, some further aspects of its nature can be affirmed by faith.

[13] I Cor. 15:53-57.

It is a realm in loving fellowship with God, in which for the Christian the love of God becomes more rich and meaningful and his response to that love more vital and untrammeled. The phrase "God's nearer presence," though not to be taken spatially, expresses this sense of more intimate communion.

Eternal life may well be conceived not only as a sphere of closer fellowship with God in Christ but with one another. The question most often in the heart, if not on the lips, of a person recently bereaved is, "Will I see and know him there?" There is no reason to doubt that the answer is Yes. Both because personality always exists in a society—the human individual would not be a person on any other basis—and because the love and the goodness of God can be trusted to minister to this deep desire of the human heart, we can look forward to fellowship with our loved ones. Without the bodily limitations and anxieties it is possible to look forward to a richer happiness in their presence in heaven than on earth.

In closer fellowship with God, "then face to face," we can hope to have knowledge of much that is now hidden from us. No omniscience that would equate our wisdom with God's can be expected or desired, but clearer knowledge of how He guides and guards our lives and of what He asks in obedient service is a reasonable hope.

By faith we may look forward to growth in love and to the expression of this love for God and for one another in service. The forms of service must, indeed, be different from those in this world of physical structures and natural necessities, but its spirit need not be different from that in which Christ has bidden us to minister. For reasons already suggested, eternity is not best conceived as a realm of static inactivity. It is reasonable to anticipate that, within the wider continuity of personal existence, the work God gives us to do will bear some relation to our talent and creativity on earth. Its precise nature, of course, it is idle to attempt to predict. That, like much else, we must be content to leave to the wisdom and the goodness of God.

To speak of growth in love and the doing of works of service to others suggests, from one point of view, incompleteness. Traditional thought has conceived of heaven as a realm of utter perfection, in which there was no need for further growth or ministry but only for praise to the Almighty in a mighty chorus of adoration. The note of praise and thanksgiving, certainly, is appropriate to the eternal life as to the present. But is this all? God is praised by deeds as well as words. And since eternal life, as the Gospel of John makes clear, begins in the present life, it cannot be wholly different. Here we find our richest satisfactions in loving service and the endeavor by God's help to "grow in the grace and knowledge of our Lord and Savior Jesus Christ." May we not believe by faith that the life beyond death also holds something of this high endeavor?

Yet from another standpoint eternal life means fulfillment, the completion of meaning, the unraveling of earth's tangles, the disclosure of ends previously but dimly apprehended. Not only is eternity the sphere of God's ultimate triumph over evil, as Christian faith has long maintained, but by His grace it is the sphere of our victory also. "Be faithful unto death, and I will give you the crown of life" (Rev. 2:10), is not simply a word spoken long ago to encourage persecuted Christians; it is God's word to Christ's followers today.

Said Paul, our "slight momentary affliction" is preparing for us an eternal weight of glory beyond all comparison (II Cor. 4:17). Often enough the affliction that assails human life is neither slight nor momentary; it is deep, heavy, long drawn out until it seems too much for human endurance. It is precisely in this situation that Paul's affirmation of hope becomes most meaningful, "for the things that are seen are transient, but the things that are unseen are eternal."

It is often said that eternal life is needed to rectify the injustices of the present life and so to solve that aspect of the problem of evil which centers in human inequalities of fate and fortune. I do not deny this aspect of it; in the long look factors may be discerned that place things in a truer perspective than is now visible. Care must be taken not to assume that in eternity all the

185

scales will be balanced as we would have them, for the destinies of men beyond death are in wiser hands than ours. Yet with due caution it may be said that eternal life does afford a ground for belief in a cosmic justice impossible without it.

This is not its main note, however. Try as we may, we do not "solve" the problem of evil by positing eternity. The Christian's faith in God's gift of eternal life does something more needful— it gives a vision of glory in the midst of earth's darkest pain. Anything then can be endured, and the future confronted with faith and hope.

Traditionally, Christian faith has looked forward to the bliss of heaven and has sought for one's self and others to avoid the torments of hell. Though eternity from either of these angles must not be conceived crudely or hedonistically, there is a note of truth here that ought not to be surrendered. If eternal life is even approximately, by God's gift, of the nature suggested in the preceding paragraphs, it is a realm of deep and abiding joy.

We do well to center attention on the goodness of God in His gift of eternal life. But there is a darker side of the picture which must not be overlooked. Not to every man indiscriminately is the word spoken, "Well done, good and faithful servant: . . . enter into the joy of your master." Sin is real; judgment is real; the refusal of God's proffered redemption is a stark reality. For those who reject God's grace, not the flames of a fiery hell but the deeper hell of remorse, of loneliness, of the utter desolation of having separated one's self from the loving presence of God may be the penalty. *Kairos* is real. The decisions made on earth matter in eternity.

Therefore, as we look toward the journey's end we need to do so with great seriousness. Death, whether for ourselves or others, is nothing about which to be flippant, indifferent, or callous. We may well believe that God desires us to delay its coming if we can, and while life lasts make life not only more tolerable but more rich in those treasures of the spirit of which our Lord has taught us. We may well believe that both glory and judgment are real and that God is ever saying to us, "You must choose."

186

Of all the milestones we must pass in life's journey, death is the most decisive.

Yet whether death comes early or late, by long anticipation or with great suddenness, the Christian who trusts the providence of God need have no fear of it. Without morbidity or undue desire he may not only anticipate it calmly but look forward to it as a great adventure—the passage by God's leading into new realms of fellowship, usefulness, and joy.

When the perishable puts on the imperishable, and the mortal puts on immortality, then shall come to pass the saying that is written:
"Death is swallowed up in victory."
"O death, where is thy victory?
O death, where is thy sting?"
(*I Cor. 15:54-55.*)

The victory of God! That, as I see it, is what the providence of God means, whether in time or eternity. "Eye hath not seen, nor ear heard, neither have entered into the heart of man, the things which God hath prepared for them that love him." Among the vicissitudes and anxieties of the earthly scene, of this we may be confident, that the Lord of time and eternity will guide and guard us still.

INDEX

Finished Sept, 1960